THE HELICOPTER

HISTORY, PILOTING AND HOW IT FLIES

BY

JOHN FAY

ILLUSTRATED BY

LUCY RAYMOND
DAVID GIBBINGS
DULCIE LEGG

DAVID & CHARLES

NEWTON ABBOT   LONDON   NORTH POMFRET (VT)   VANCOUVER

ISBN 0 7153 7249 1

First published as *The Helicopter and How It Flies* 1954 by Pitman Publishing. Third edition, revised and with additional chapter, published by David & Charles as *The Helicopter: History, Piloting and How It Flies* 1976

Printed in Great Britain
by Redwood Burn Limited Trowbridge and Esher
for David & Charles (Publishers) Limited
Brunel House Newton Abbot Devon

Published in the United States of America
by David & Charles Inc
North Pomfret Vermont 05053 USA

Published in Canada
by Douglas David & Charles Limited
1875 Welch Street North Vancouver BC

To

MY WIFE

PREFACE TO THE THIRD EDITION

In this edition I have made several alterations to the existing text and have added a chapter on helicopter history. I have now retired from flying, but I am fortunate in having a fount of rotary-wing knowledge right on my doorstep in the form of my old firm Westland Helicopters Ltd, and I must thank them for their help and for the use of their facilities, without which it would have been difficult to obtain the necessary information. It would have been impossible, however, to have achieved any degree of authenticity without the aid of the people mentioned below, and my thanks to them is but a small return for that assistance.

First, David Gibbings, who followed in the footsteps of the late Lucy Raymond and produced most of the excellent illustrations found in the new chapter. As a flight engineer he was eminently suited to the task of reading into contemporary photographs and drawings features which were not always readily discernible. He was also invaluable in that he was able to obtain many items of information that I might otherwise have missed. Then, L. H. Hayward, who, as a patents engineer, was just the right sort of person to approach for advice or documents concerning some of the earlier helicopters. The lecture he gave some years ago on helicopter patents was a useful reference and is worth further study by students. Next, G. A. Elsmore, R. A. C. Brie and John W. R. Taylor for assistance with some of the items.

The following, without whose assistance certain sections would have been lacking in many respects: O. Fitzwilliams, D. E. H. Balmford, A. L. Carnegie, and my former colleagues K. H. Chadbourn, R. R. Crayton, J. Morton, R. Moxam and P. D. R. Wilson.

The following organizations and people for their help or for giving me permission to quote from the works mentioned: The British Museum, and especially Miss Yu-ying of the Department of Oriental Printed Books and Manuscripts; Her Majesty's Stationery Office: *Aviation* by Charles Gibbs-Smith; The Royal Aeronautical Society: publications by the Helicopter Association of Great Britain and articles in the *Journal* of the Royal Aeronautical Society; Cambridge University Press: *Science and Civilisation in China*, by Joseph Needham; I. P. C. Transport Press Ltd: *Flight International*, and last but by no means least, the Blandford Press and Kenneth Munson, not only because the book *Helicopters and other Rotorcraft Since 1907* was a valuable source of information, but also for permission to redraw in black and white five colour pictures from that work painted by John W. Wood.

Finally, let us spare a thought for those who make aviation history, especially those early pioneers who, despite years of effort, never fulfilled their dream of controlled hovering flight in a heavier-than-air machine. It was through the collective zeal and dedication of many of these men that others were able to attain that goal in later years.

J.F.

PREFACE TO THE FIRST EDITION

FROM the remarks of many people in the past few years, it has become apparent that a simple book is needed which will give basic information about helicopter theory without the frills of a more technical publication. This country is now becoming helicopter minded, and an increasing number of people who have hitherto been concerned only with fixed-wing aircraft are becoming associated with rotary-wing aircraft. It is hoped that this book will supply much of the initial information required and that it will also serve as a foundation for those who wish to go into matters in more detail.

The errors of a book which attempts to simplify any subject are usually ones of slight inaccuracy. I have done my best to avoid these pitfalls, although it may be thought by some that certain aspects have been dismissed rather briefly. These people are referred to the many excellent works which approach the subject in a much more erudite fashion and which contain a wealth of mathematical formulae to add to their attraction.

My grateful thanks are due to my friend Mr. A. McClements for giving me the right course to steer soon after take-off, and to Captain J. A. Cameron, Mr. L. M. Cohen, Mr. C. C.

Cooper, Mr. R. Hafner, Mr. G. Hinchliffe, Mr. F. O'Hara, Mr. W. Stewart, and Mr. A. H. Yates who gave me assistance in many different ways in order to keep me on track, and especially to my colleagues Mr. A. L. Carnegie and Mr. J. Speechley for their guidance and to Mr. O. L. L. Fitzwilliams who was my final approach on any doubtful matters. I must also thank Mrs. N. MacMillan for some of the typing, and last, but not least, Miss Lucy Raymond for the way in which she translated my untidy scribbles into such excellent illustrations.

J. F.

CONTENTS

CHAPTER VIII

CHAPTER I

INTRODUCTION TO THE HELICOPTER

Definitions

Rotor   A system of rotating aerofoils.

Rotorcraft   An aerodyne which throughout all or part of its flight derives the whole or part of its lift from a rotor or rotors rotating in a substantially horizontal plane.

Gyroplane (also known as *autogyro*)   A rotorcraft which throughout its flight derives the whole or a substantial part of its lift from a freely-rotating rotor.

Helicopter   A rotorcraft deriving the whole or a substantial part of its lift from one or more power-driven rotors.

Compound Helicopter   A rotorcraft, the rotating wings of which supply at all times during flight a substantial part of the lift, but which in addition embodies aerodynamic components such as wings and/or propellers that, mainly at higher translational speeds, supplement the action of the rotating wings.

Convertiplane   A powered rotorcraft which is capable of conversion during flight so that the lift is substantially or totally transferred from the rotor(s) to fixed wings and vice versa.

Since the distinction between a *helicopter* and a *compound helicopter* may depend largely upon opinions regarding the size of the fixed wings, a helicopter without wings and with no extra propulsion aids is sometimes called a *pure helicopter*.

Genealogical Tree

Together with lighter-than-air machines and aeroplanes, rotorcraft come under the general heading of *aircraft* and their place in the genealogical tree (Fig. 1) shows how they are related.

1

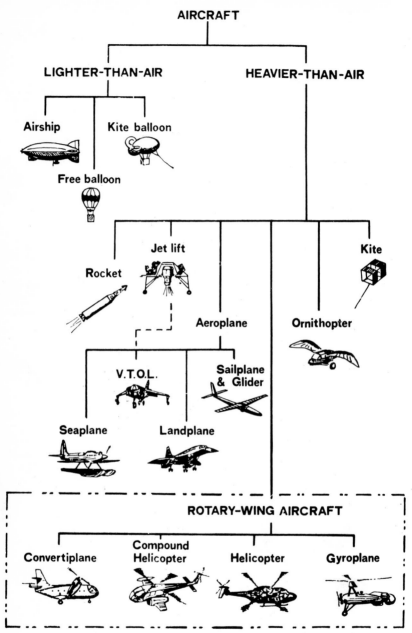

FIG. 1. THE GENEALOGICAL TREE OF AIRCRAFT

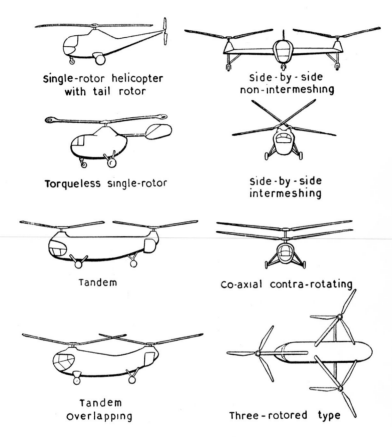

Single-rotor helicopter
with tail rotor

side-by-side
non-intermeshing

Torqueless single-rotor

side-by-side
intermeshing

Tandem

Co-axial contra-rotating

Tandem
overlapping

Three-rotored type

FIG. 2. SOME HELICOPTER CONFIGURATIONS

3

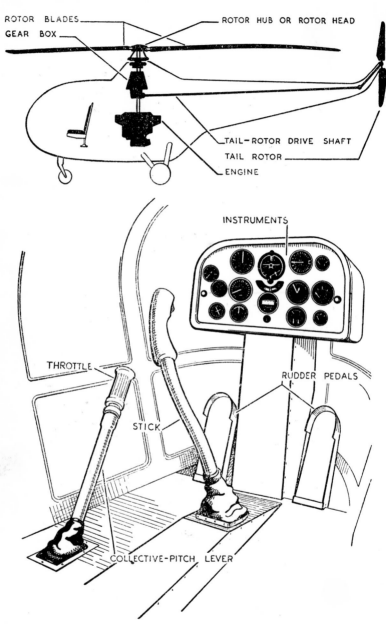

FIG 3. SOME FEATURES OF THE HELICOPTER AND COCKPIT

4

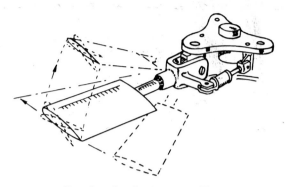

FIG. 4A. AN ARTICULATED ROTOR

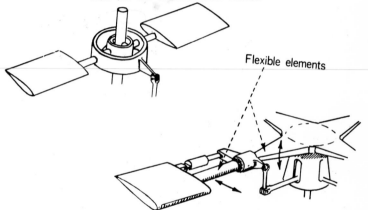

Flexible elements

FIG. 4B. SEMI-RIGID ROTORS

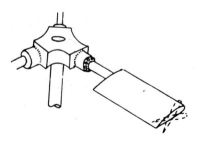

FIG. 4C. A FULLY RIGID ROTOR

5

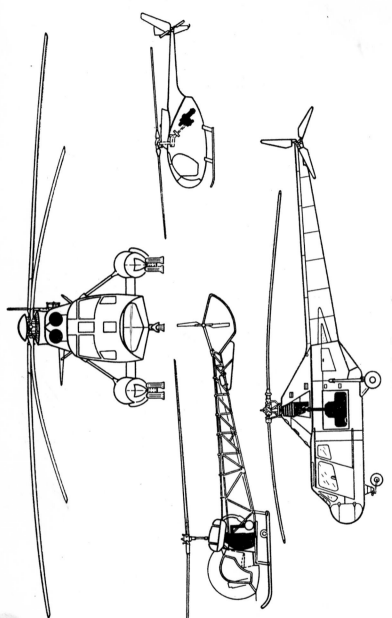

FIG. 5. ENGINE LOCATIONS

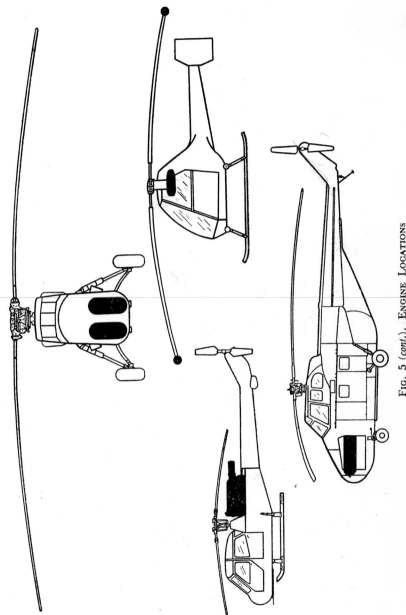

FIG. 5 (cont.). ENGINE LOCATIONS

Some helicopter configurations are shown in Fig. 2 and the main parts of the helicopter are illustrated in Fig. 3.

In this book, the single-rotor helicopter is the one which is mainly discussed, for not only is it the most common type, but the theory of the multi-rotor helicopter is basically similar.

Types of Rotor

Rotors may also be divided into types. An *articulated* rotor (Fig. 4A) is one in which the individual blades are free to flap, drag and change pitch. This is made possible by mounting the blades on flapping and drag hinges and pitch-change bearings. The term *semi-rigid* (Fig. 4B) is often used to denote a rotor in which the blades are without individual flapping and drag hinges; the blades can, however, flap like a see-saw about a central gimbal. The term is now applied more generally to rotors whose blades have roots that are designed to flex in the flapping and drag planes: this is not apparent at a casual glance but the fact that drag dampers may be fitted will help in identification. A *rigid* rotor (Fig. 4C) is one in which the blades are free to change pitch but otherwise are made as rigid as possible.

Rotors normally have two or more blades. Six blades to a rotor is the maximum in use at present.

Rotor blades are aerofoils and can be of metal, wood, plastic or composite construction.

Engines

Helicopters can have their rotors shaft driven by piston engines or gas turbines, or can have tip-jet drive by various types of engines. Examples of engine locations are shown in Fig. 5.

Undercarriages

The undercarriage of a helicopter can consist of wheels, skids or floats; or the aircraft can have a flying-boat hull. Some land helicopters are fitted with inflatable flotation gear for emergency landings on water. Many helicopters now have retractable undercarriages.

CHAPTER II

THE HELICOPTER IN VERTICAL POWERED FLIGHT

THE THEORY

In order that any object may leave the ground, an upward force which is greater than the weight must be applied to it.

Weight and Lift

In Fig. 6 vectors representing lift and weight have been drawn. Note that the lift vector is longer than the weight

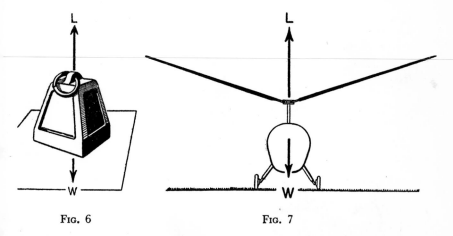

Fig. 6   Fig. 7

vector. While it remains so, the body will accelerate upwards (if we ignore drag).

If we make the lift equal to the weight, the body will remain in equilibrium.

To make a helicopter rise from the ground (Fig. 7), we must apply an upward force to the rotor head, which, in a single-rotor helicopter, is situated above the centre of gravity. The applied force must be slightly greater than the weight of the helicopter.

Initial power is supplied by the engine, and the engine

9

turns the rotor blades. These aerofoils move through the air in much the same way as the wing of an aeroplane, except that they rotate instead of moving only forwards. We know that the wings of a fixed-wing aircraft must have an angle of attack to produce any appreciable lifting force, and it is the same with the rotating wings of a helicopter. The blades can

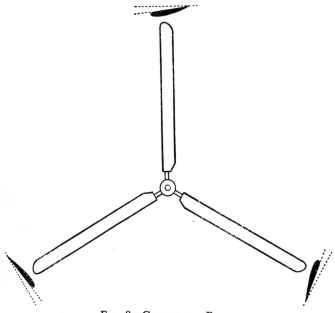

Fig. 8. Collective Pitch

be rotated very fast, but until the pilot gives the blades a certain amount of pitch as in Fig. 8 (in this case *collective* pitch as all the blades will change pitch equally and in the same direction) by moving one of his controls, no effective lift force will be produced and the helicopter will not rise. In present helicopters the mean collective-pitch angle can be varied from approximately 3° to 14°.

When the collective pitch of the blades has been increased, and provided the rotor has sufficient rotational speed, air is forced downwards and the blades tend to lift themselves upwards, with the helicopter to which they are attached.

Methods of Varying Lift

Once the blades of a given helicopter have a certain amount of pitch, the amount of lift they give depends on the angle of attack (within certain limits) and the square of the speed of the blades (Figs. 9A and 9B).

In theory, therefore, either the revolutions per minute (r.p.m.) or the pitch angle of the blades can be changed in order to vary the amount of lift. But it takes time to alter the speed of the rotor because it has considerable inertia. In

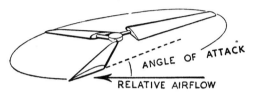

FIG. 9A. LIFT VARIES WITH ANGLE OF ATTACK

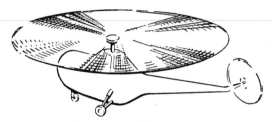

FIG. 9B. LIFT CAN BE VARIED WITH R.P.M.

practice, the r.p.m. are retained within certain limits by use of the throttle and, in general, only the pitch of the blades is altered.

Reasons for Varying Collective Pitch

Apart from varying the thrust of the rotor independently of the rotor speed, changes in collective pitch are required to compensate for the change in air density with altitude, and to compensate for the changes in angle of attack due to variations in axial flow in translational flight.

The Lift Vector

The separate lifting force of each blade can be represented by a small vector, but for convenience the separate vectors of each blade are usually combined into one resultant vector acting at the centre of the rotor (Fig. 10).

In a hovering helicopter, the force represented by this vector is equal to the weight of the aircraft. If the force is increased, the helicopter will rise; if it is decreased, gravity will cause the machine to descend (Fig. 11).

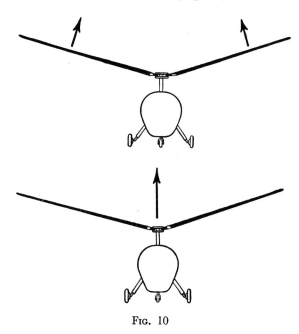

Fig. 10

Twisted and Tapered Blades

The lift of an aerofoil varies as the square of the speed. Hence in a rotor blade which is neither twisted nor tapered, the lift along the blade will vary as the square of the radius (apart from some loss of lift at the tip similar to the loss of lift in a fixed-wing aircraft due to wing-tip vortices).

The lift of an aerofoil is gained by imparting a downward momentum to particles of air, and the inflow of air to the blade in Fig. 12 will vary considerably along the span. The ideal is for the inflow to be constant along the span, and in order to achieve this, blades can be constructed with a twist

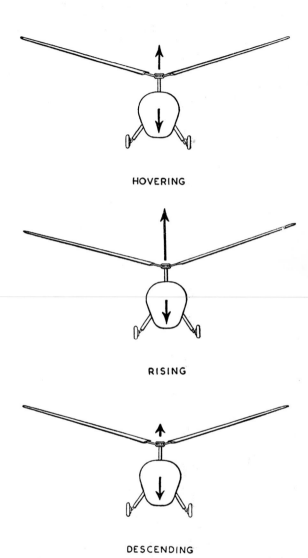

HOVERING

RISING

DESCENDING

FIG. 11. VERTICAL MOVEMENT FROM THE HOVER

or taper (Fig. 13). Lift then can be made to vary as the radius (apart from tip-loss effect), which is the desirable condition.

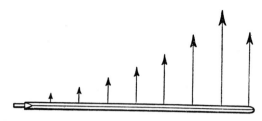

FIG. 12. LIFT DISTRIBUTION ALONG THE SPAN OF A
PARALLEL-SECTION NON-TWISTED BLADE

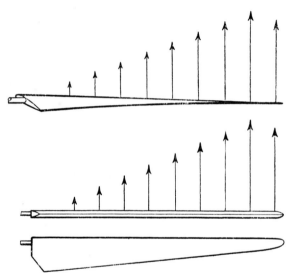

FIG. 13. LIFT DISTRIBUTION ALONG THE SPAN OF
TWISTED OR TAPERED BLADES

Airflow Patterns

Let us now look at the airflow pattern diagrams of a helicopter hovering in calm air (Fig. 14A), and that of a helicopter when it is in the *vortex ring state* (Fig. 14B). The latter term is derived from the fact that a ring of air is formed round the rotor blades. In this condition, the helicopter will encounter turbulence and the pilot will experience vibration, a high rate of sink and some partial loss of control due to the fact that the helicopter is descending into its own slipstream.

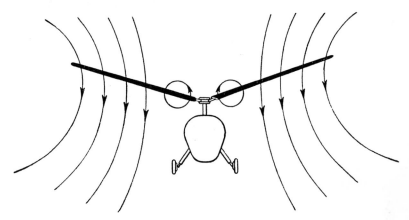

FIG. 14A. AIRFLOW PATTERN OF HELICOPTER WHEN HOVERING

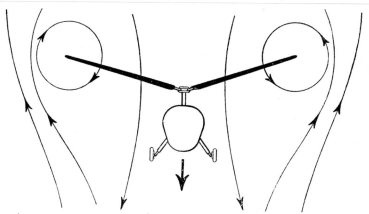

FIG. 14B. AIRFLOW PATTERN OF HELICOPTER IN VORTEX RING STATE, A CONDITION SOMETIMES MET DURING VERTICAL POWERED DESCENTS

THE PILOT'S CONTROL FOR LIFT

We will now see how the helicopter controls are arranged in order to bring about alterations of rotor thrust by changes of collective pitch and changes of rotor speed.

Changing Blade Pitch

The requirement is to take a blade and mount it in such a manner that it will pivot about its pitch-change axis. We could grasp the blade shown in Fig. 15 at either the leading edge or the trailing edge, which for convenience we will do at the point T, and by moving it up and down we could produce changes of pitch angle.

If we attach a rod to the point T or a similar position, and by means of cranks and levers lead a control linkage to the cockpit, we could give the pilot something to push or pull in

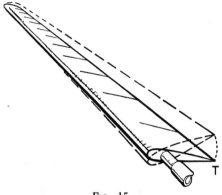

FIG. 15

order to change the pitch angle at will. At present, helicopters have a lever (Fig. 16) which is generally held in the left hand and which is arranged so that, when it is pulled up, the pitch angles of all the blades go up—and so does the helicopter if the rotor is going round fast enough.

This lever is called the *collective-pitch* lever because it changes the pitch of all the blades of the rotor simultaneously and in the same direction. Instead of "lever" some people refer to it as the "stick," but since this is the name of another of the helicopter controls, dangerous confusion could be caused when carrying out flying training.

Although the normal means of changing the pitch of the blades is by pivoting the blades on bearings, there is another method in use whereby the blades themselves are made flexible torsionally, pitch-change bearings not being fitted. By changing the pitch of an aileron, tab, or servo flap,

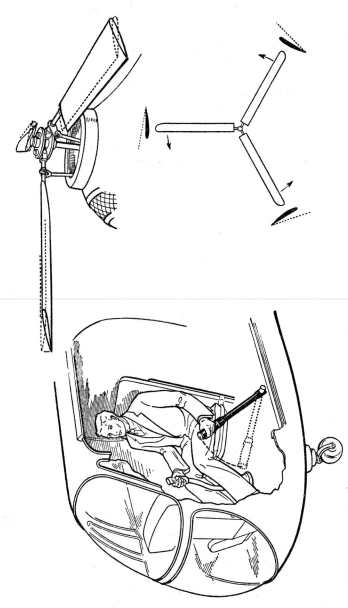

Fig. 16. Pulling the Collective-pitch Lever up will increase Blade Pitch equally on all the Blades

which is mounted on the trailing edge near the tip, the blade can be twisted during flight and a change of pitch effected. Alternatively, the aileron can be large in proportion to the

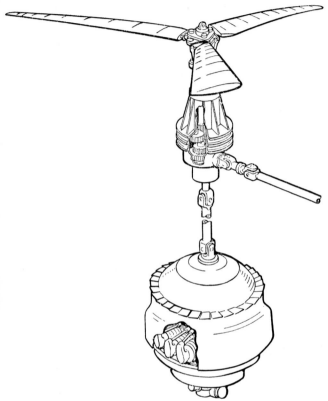

FIG. 17. A TYPICAL LAYOUT OF PISTON ENGINE, GEAR-BOX AND ROTOR

rest of the blade, which is torsionally stiff and serves as a mounting for the aileron. A change of aileron angle is similar to a change of pitch angle of a normal blade.

Changing the Rotor Speed in Piston-engined Helicopters

The engine is arranged in such a manner that it will drive the rotor through a gear-box. A typical arrangement is shown in Fig. 17.

The Twist-grip Throttle

To vary the speed of the rotor, the pilot must have control over the engine speed, and the normal type of throttle is the "twist-grip" type which is mounted on the end of the collective-pitch lever.

FIG. 18. THE TWIST-GRIP THROTTLE

Automatic Throttle Changes

For large alterations of blade pitch, big changes of throttle opening are necessary to maintain a given rotor speed because of the variations in blade drag. In order to take some of the work from the pilot, a simple device is fitted to the collective-pitch control system. When collective pitch is increased, a system of levers automatically opens the throttle (or appropriate method of increasing the fuel mixture to the engine) in the carburettor, and closes it as necessary when the collective-pitch lever is pushed down, the position of the throttle control in the pilot's hand not being affected. With good adjustment of this device, which is generally in the form of a cam, the pilot is relieved of much concentration, although some adjustment of the hand control is often necessary in any change of flight condition in order to keep constant r.p.m.

Rotor Speed Governing in Gas Turbine Helicopters

Helicopters with shaft-driven rotors and gas turbine engines generally have an automatic system of rotor r.p.m. control in powered flight. The pilot's twist-grip throttle is dispensed

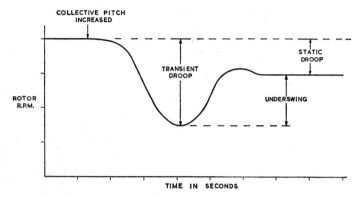

FIG. 19. TRANSIENT DROOP AND STATIC DROOP FOLLOWING A FAIRLY RAPID INCREASE IN COLLECTIVE PITCH

with, although it may be available as an emergency manual control or as a speed select control, depending on the helicopter type. With automatic rotor speed governing, the desired rotor r.p.m. band is selected by the pilot prior to take-off. The fuel flow is then automatically controlled to maintain the rotor r.p.m. within a correct and safe range during all normal conditions of powered flight, despite changes of collective pitch made by the pilot.

Transient and Static Droop

The majority of automatic systems do not hold the rotor r.p.m. at a fixed figure for all conditions of powered flight. The problems of automatic r.p.m. control and r.p.m. stability are simplified if the rotor r.p.m. are in the lower section of the r.p.m. band for high power and in the higher section of the r.p.m. range for low power.

When the pilot increases collective pitch within the normal powered flight range, the rotor r.p.m. will tend to fall despite an increase in fuel flow and power. The initial total fall in rotor r.p.m. is called *transient droop*. The transient droop can be small or comparatively large depending upon the rate and amount by which the collective-pitch lever is raised. After a small time-lag, automatic governing will tend to stabilize the r.p.m. at a new figure which will be lower than the stabilized figure obtained prior to the collective-pitch change. The change in stabilized r.p.m. is referred to as *static droop*.

The r.p.m. difference between transient droop and static droop is called the *underswing*.

Static Droop Cancelling

The greater the static droop the greater is the rotor r.p.m. stability. Hence it might be thought desirable to have a large static droop. However, this might affect the performance of some helicopters and it is necessary to reduce the static droop. This is usually achieved by taking a position signal from the collective-pitch lever and feeding it into the automatic system in order progressively to change the static droop datum. This is called *static droop cancelling* and with it the static droop can be reduced to negligible proportions.

Cockpit Instruments

The basic flight instruments in the cockpit are similar to those in a fixed-wing aircraft. There are no instruments to inform the pilot of sideways or backwards airspeeds. Forward airspeed is shown by the familiar Air-Speed Indicator (A.S.I.) as used in aeroplanes. One instrument is more complex, however, and that is the engine-rotor tachometer or r.p.m. gauge. In the helicopter the tachometer is two instruments with one clock face. The long needle indicates the rotor r.p.m. on an outer scale and the short needle indicates the engine needle on an inner scale. (*Note.* American practice is to have the engine needle on the outer scale and the rotor needle on the inner scale.) The calibration of the gauge is such that when the clutch between engine and transmission is fully engaged the two needles are superimposed. The information supplied by the two needles in various representative conditions can be illustrated by the following examples—

A. Engine started and idling at 1,000 r.p.m.

B. Clutch being engaged. The engine r.p.m. have been

increased. The rotor is accelerating either because the clutch is centrifugally operated or the pilot is engaging a manual clutch.

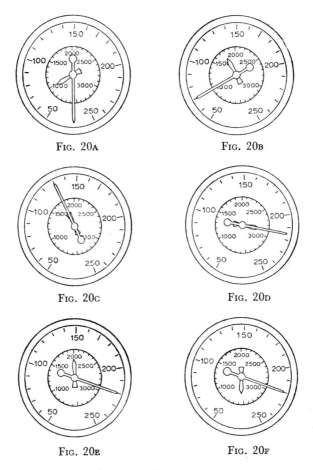

FIG. 20A   FIG. 20B

FIG. 20C   FIG. 20D

FIG. 20E   FIG. 20F

Note. Gas turbine engines have a different system. There can be a direct drive from the compressor, possibly through a clutch, to the transmission, or there may be a *free turbine* system. In this, an extra turbine disc is located at the rear of the engine and is connected directly to the transmission, but not to the remainder of the engine. Gases generated by the engine flow through the free turbine and tend to rotate it; so there is in effect a gas clutch between engine and transmission. When starting the engine, the rotor and all the transmission, including the free turbine, can be held by the rotor brake. Rotor engagement can be made when desired by releasing the rotor brake and accelerating the engine.

C. Clutch fully engaged.

D. Normal flight condition.

E. Gliding flight (autorotation). The engine is idling at a convenient speed and the rotor is being driven by the airflow.

F. Gliding flight (autorotation), similar to *E*, but the engine has stopped.

In twin- or multiple-engined helicopters there are two or more small needles indicating the appropriate engine r.p.m. The phrases "splitting the needles", "needles split", and "needles joined" are often used to describe the entry into autorotation, the autorotative condition and the recovery to powered flight respectively.

CHAPTER III

THE HELICOPTER IN POWERED
TRANSLATIONAL FLIGHT

THE THEORY

THE propeller-driven fixed-wing aircraft moves forward by pushing the air backwards with its propeller, the equal and opposite reaction forcing the aircraft forwards. The true

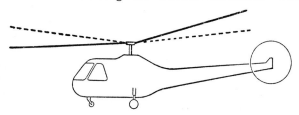

FIG. 21. ROTOR TILTED FOR FORWARD FLIGHT

helicopter has no separate propeller to provide forward propulsion. It does move forward by pushing the air backwards, however, and this is carried out by forward tilt of the rotor disc from the horizontal (Fig. 21). (The imaginary surface swept by the rotor blades during their rotation is often referred to as a disc.)

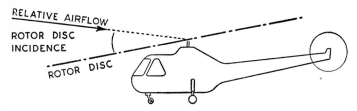

FIG. 22A. ROTOR DISC INCIDENCE

Tilting the Lift Vector

Notice that although the rotor disc may be tilted in relation to the fuselage, the drive shaft does not tilt except with changes

24

of fuselage attitude. The angle between the relative airflow
and the rotor disc is called *rotor disc incidence* (Fig. 22A) and the

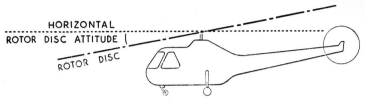

HORIZONTAL

ROTOR DISC ATTITUDE

ROTOR DISC

FIG. 22B. ROTOR DISC ATTITUDE

angle between the rotor disc and the horizontal is called *rotor
disc attitude* (Fig. 22B). When the rotor disc is tilted, the airflow
is not only down through the rotor, but slightly backwards
as well. If we now examine the lift vector, we find that

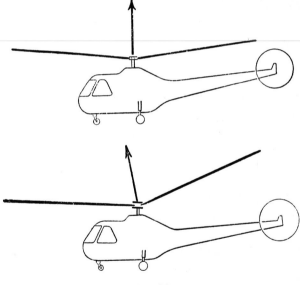

FIG. 23

instead of being vertical as it was for hovering flight it has
been inclined forward slightly (Fig. 23).

This vector can be resolved into two components representing a vertical force and a horizontal force as shown in

Fig. 24. If we now draw in the weight vector, we can see that our helicopter will accelerate forwards (Fig. 25).

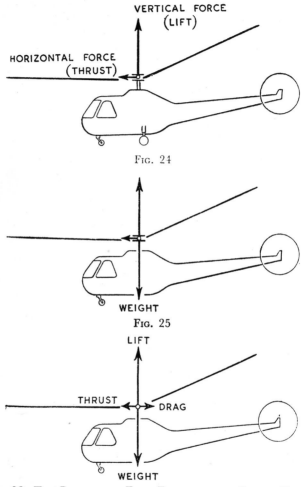

VERTICAL FORCE
(LIFT)

HORIZONTAL FORCE
(THRUST)

FIG. 24

WEIGHT

FIG. 25

LIFT

THRUST ← → DRAG

WEIGHT

FIG. 26. THE BALANCE OF FOUR FORCES DURING STEADY FLIGHT

The Balance of Four Forces

On attaining speed, drag comes into the picture. When steady flight is reached we get back to our old friend found in fixed-wing theory—the balance of four forces (Fig. 26).

Movement in any Direction

During flight, a fixed-wing aircraft banks in the required direction when a turn is carried out. The lift on the wings, in addition to supplying a sustaining force holding the aircraft in the air, supplies a component towards the centre of the turn. In exactly the same way a helicopter must bank when making a turn in forward flight.

A helicopter can move in any horizontal direction while maintaining a fixed heading, merely by tilting the rotor disc in the required direction. We have seen already that the helicopter can move vertically upwards and downwards, so by combining horizontal and vertical motions we can make our helicopter move, as has so often been said, in 362 directions—all the points of the compass and up and down as well.

Fuselage Attitude

A point to note is the varying attitude of the fuselage as the helicopter accelerates forward from the hovering position.

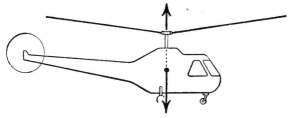

FIG. 27A. FUSELAGE ATTITUDE WHEN HOVERING

Assuming that the fuselage is level during hovering flight and that the thrust line of the main rotor passes through the c.g. of the helicopter (Fig. 27A), then when the rotor disc is tilted forward, the nose will move down owing to the forward component of the rotor thrust causing a moment about the c.g. (Fig. 27B).

This nose-down attitude will increase until the thrust line is again through the c.g. (Fig. 27C). This will occur when the forward inclination of the disc is decreased slightly.

Drag acting on the nose of the helicopter and the (normally) horizontal surfaces of the tail will also have some influence on the fuselage attitude in forward flight.

For passenger-carrying duties the nose-down attitude in forward flight is not very comfortable and one method of improvement is for the designers to arrange for the helicopter to hover in a tail-down attitude. Then in cruising flight, when the helicopter is in a more tail-up position, the fuselage will be fairly level (Fig. 28).

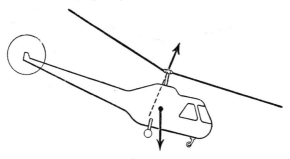

FIG. 27b. FUSELAGE ATTITUDE WHEN ACCELERATING

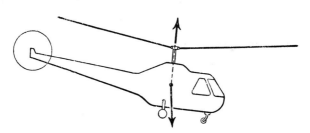

FIG. 27c. STEADY FLIGHT

Apart from the point of view of comfort, a practical advantage of having the fuselage level during forward flight is that there is less fuselage drag. Thus for the same power the cruising speed of the helicopter can be increased.

The simplest way of arranging for the helicopter to hover tail down and to fly forward in a level attitude is to have the c.g. slightly aft of the usual position. This, however, limits the amount of forward rotor inclination available. This disadvantage can be overcome by designing the helicopter with the hub and drive shaft inclined slightly forward. The arrangement will also tend to make the aircraft smoother in forward flight.

Some helicopters have adjustable surfaces fitted at the tail which can be used to trim the aircraft attitude in forward flight. In certain aircraft the inclination can be adjusted from the cockpit, in others the setting is fixed and can be adjusted on the ground only.

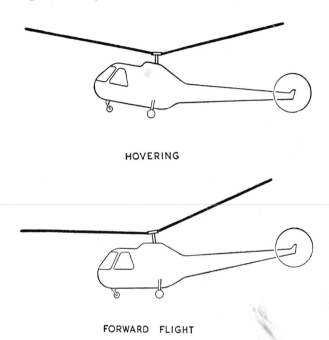

HOVERING

FORWARD FLIGHT

Fig. 28. A More Comfortable Arrangement

HOW THE ROTOR DISC IS TILTED

The more common methods for tilting the rotor disc are—

The Cyclic-pitch Method

This is the most common one in use for tilting the disc. Let us be quite clear as to the difference between *collective* and *cyclic* pitch. In a collective-pitch change, all the rotor blades change their pitch together, by the same amount, and in the same direction. In a cyclic-pitch change (sometimes called cyclic feathering), the pitch of each blade is altered consecutively from a minimum to a maximum, as determined by the position of the pilot's control, during each revolution of the

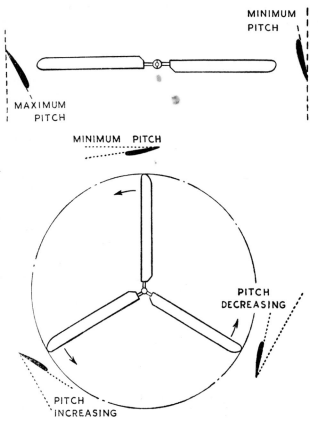

FIG. 29. CYCLIC-PITCH CHANGES

rotor. In a two-bladed rotor, therefore, the blades reach maximum and minimum pitch positions respectively at one particular instant (Fig. 29). In the case of the three-bladed rotor, if one blade is passing through the minimum pitch position the other two would be in the process of increasing and decreasing their pitch respectively.

Now, to tilt the rotor disc forward for forward flight, the blade which happens to be moving round towards the rear of

the disc must be caused to ride up so as to be at its highest
position at the rear of the disc. Conversely, the blade which
happens to be moving round towards the front must be
caused to ride lower so that it is at its lowest position when in
the front of the disc. The blades are free to move up and down
on hinges or flexible blade root elements, and they can be
caused to ride up or down by giving them more or less lift in
their appropriate position round the circle.

Note that, in translational flight, the blade moving forward

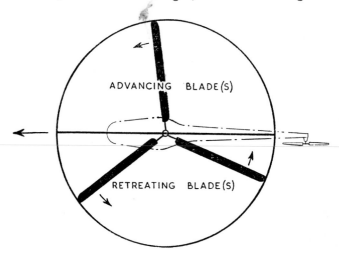

FIG. 30. ADVANCING AND RETREATING BLADES

into the relative airflow is called the *advancing* blade. On moving
into the opposite sector it becomes the *retreating* blade (Fig.
30).

To give an individual blade more or less lift is merely a
matter of giving it more or less pitch as it rotates—giving it,
in fact, a cyclic-pitch change (Figs. 31A and 31B). The retreating blade is given an increase in pitch and the advancing
blade is given a decrease in pitch; the rotor disc then tilts
itself forward for forward flight.

Naturally any changes of cyclic pitch are superimposed on
the mean collective pitch, and the total lift force will therefore
remain substantially the same.

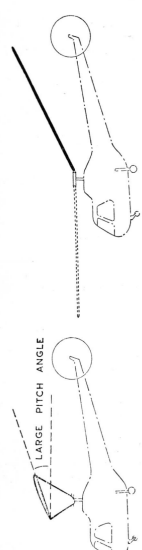

LARGE PITCH ANGLE

FIG. 31A. AN INCREASE IN PITCH ANGLE CAUSES A BLADE TO RISE

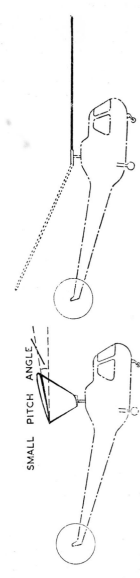

SMALL PITCH ANGLE

FIG. 31B. A DECREASE IN PITCH ANGLE CAUSES A BLADE TO FALL

Tilting-hub Method

This method was used in the Cierva Autogiros, but in the power-driven rotors of the helicopter certain difficulties would be encountered and the method is not common. In the tilting-hub system (Figs. 32A to c), the whole hub to which the blades are attached is tilted. The rotor disc follows suit, not because the blades are forced to rise or fall by the

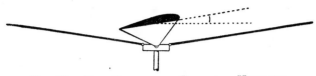

FIG. 32A. THE TILTING-HUB CONTROL: HOVERING

FIG. 32B. THE TILTING-HUB CONTROL: THE MOMENTARY CONDITION WHEN THE HUB IS TILTED

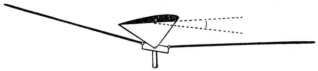

FIG. 32C. THE TILTING-HUB CONTROL: THE NEW ATTITUDE OF THE ROTOR DISC

hub to which they are attached, but because when the hub is inclined a cyclic-pitch change of the blades takes place and the change in aerodynamic lift on the individual blades makes them rise or fall, as in the normal cyclic-pitch system.

Moving the c.g. System

If the fuselage, and therefore the rotor hub, of a helicopter can be tilted independently of the rotor, the rotor disc will follow suit just as in the tilting-hub system. The fuselage, and therefore the rotor disc, can be tilted by altering the position of the c.g. during flight. This method of control has been used with some success in a helicopter in which movement of the stick caused the pilot's cockpit to move. The disadvantages of the system are that it has a time lag in operation, and that it must be restricted to small helicopters.

Flapping

Blades ride higher and lower during their rotation, but they can only do this if they are allowed to move freely about a horizontal hinge or flexible root element; or, in other words,

FIG. 33A. A ROTOR BLADE FLAPPING ABOUT A HINGE

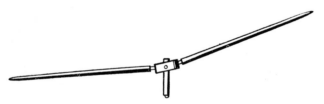

FIG. 33B. THE FLAPPING OF A GIMBAL-MOUNTED ROTOR
(NOTE THE BUILT-IN CONING ANGLE)

can *flap*. Accordingly each blade can move vertically about an axis at its root, either independently or on a central gimbal. Where individual hinges are fitted they are referred to as *flapping hinges* (Fig. 33A). The definition of flapping is: "The angular oscillation of a rotor blade about a substantially horizontal axis." Flapping hinges are usually set at 90° to the span of the blade, but some are set at an angle (see *delta-three hinge*, page 104).

In the case of the gimbal-mounted rotor the blades move like a see-saw about the gimbal (Fig. 33B).

Note that flapping motion is the result of the cyclical change of balance between the lift, centrifugal, and inertia forces, and that while the rotor is maintaining any substantially fixed plane the resultant of these forces acting on each blade root will be equal. It is only when the resultants are momentarily unequal, owing to, say, a stick movement, that the plane of the rotor disc will alter.

THE PHASE LAG

When an increase in pitch is given to a rotor blade, the blade does not immediately rise to a high flapped position, but does so up to 90° later in its revolution. In Fig. 34 it is required to tilt the disc forward, so the stick (not shown) is placed forward. When any blade reaches position A it is given a maximum pitch. But the blade does not reach its highest flapped position until it is over the tail of the aircraft.

In a similar way the blade is given a minimum pitch in a position 180° from where it received the maximum pitch, but only reaches its lowest flapped position over the nose of the aircraft 90° later.

With the blades flapping high over the tail and low over the nose of the aircraft, the rotor disc is effectively tilted for forward flight.

Inertia

We may wonder why the blade does not flap immediately in direct relation to the degree of pitch. For instance, given a

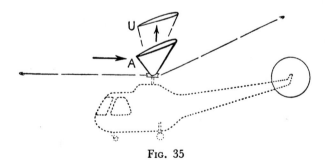

Fig. 35

large degree of pitch at point A, Fig. 35, why does not the blade immediately rise to the point U shown above?

It is because of the inertia of the blade. The blade cannot

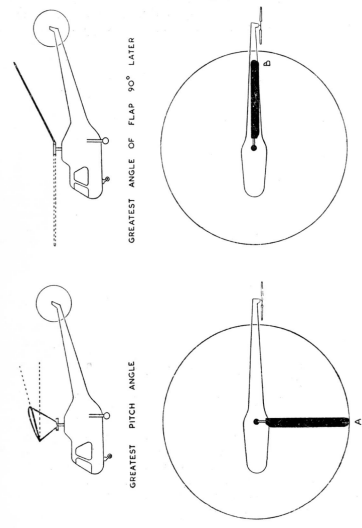

GREATEST ANGLE OF FLAP 90° LATER

GREATEST PITCH ANGLE

B

A

FIG. 34. THE PHASE-LAG FOLLOWING A PITCH CHANGE

immediately lose, in this case, its rearward motion and shoot off at right angles to its original path. In proof of this try swinging your arm (and body) around horizontally and then try lifting your arm vertically upwards. You will find that by

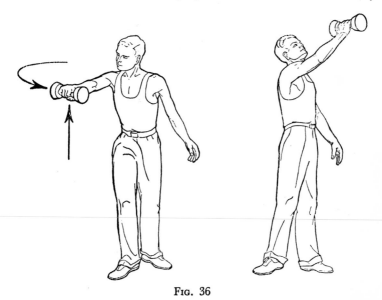

FIG. 36

the time it has reached a reasonably high position it will be well past the place at which you started to lift it.

This experiment is even more convincing if a weight is held in the hand (Fig. 36).

In the helicopter rotor the phase lag depends on how far out (i.e. the amount of offset) from the centre of the rotor the flapping hinges are situated. In the normal rotors with slightly off-set hinges the phase lag is usually between 80° and 90°. The offset is not always small, however, and some success-ful helicopters have flapping hinges situated about half-way along the blades.

The Effect on Control of Off-set Flapping Hinges

One of the advantages of off-set flapping hinges is the fact that a dynamic effect, distinct from an aerodynamic effect, is

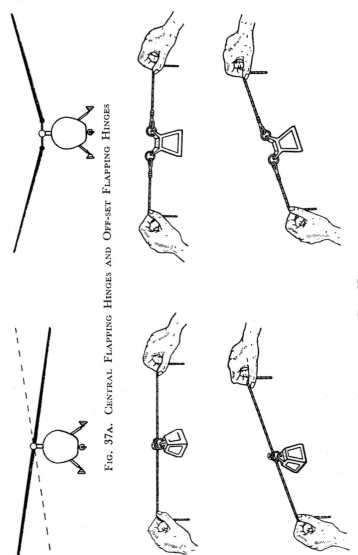

FIG. 37A. CENTRAL FLAPPING HINGES AND OFF-SET FLAPPING HINGES

FIG. 37B

produced on the fuselage. The fuselage will, therefore, follow any rotor disc tilt more quickly and the pilot will have a more sensitive control.

In a helicopter with rotor blades flapping about the rotor centre the basic factor affecting the fuselage attitude in flight is the change in direction of the lift vector, but where off-set hinges are fitted the fuselage is caused to tilt by dynamic means as well. Naturally, however, the dynamic effect cannot be obtained without the initial flapping displacement of the rotor blades caused by aerodynamic means.

We can illustrate the dynamic effect caused by off-set flapping hinges by using a piece of string attached to a weight (representing the fuselage) by a single point, which is equivalent to a rotor system with central flapping hinges; and then by attaching another piece of string to a weight by two separate points, which is equivalent to a rotor system with off-set flapping hinges.

Provided the string is kept taut, the first weight will not tilt with the string movements as shown in Fig. 37B whereas the second weight will immediately follow the string movements owing to the couple (see p. 52) created.

The distance the flapping hinges are offset from the rotor centre will naturally affect the magnitude of the dynamic couple.

In a rigid rotor system the extremely stiff coupling between rotor and fuselage will have a similar effect to that of widely off-set flapping hinges.

Gyroscopic Precession

In a rotor in which the blades flap about a central gimbal and are pivoted at the geometric centre of the rotor, the rotor will behave in a similar way to a gyroscope. One of the laws of gyroscopics states that, when a couple is applied to a gyroscope, the gyroscope will tilt or precess in the plane at right angles to the plane containing the couple (Fig. 38). You can prove this to yourself with one of the gyroscopes sold in toyshops. Spin it and then give it a quick push with the finger. It will immediately tilt at right angles to the direction of the push.

Some rotors can therefore be said to behave like a gyroscope in that their phase-lag is 90°.

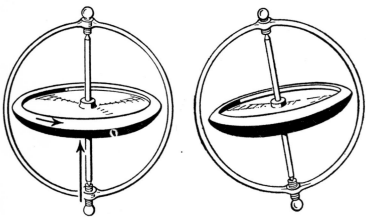

FIG. 38. GYROSCOPIC PRECESSION

Maintaining Planes of Rotation

A rotor will tend to maintain a new plane of rotation so long as the force on the blades does not alter. Although we know that the angles of attack of the blades are continually changing during rotation, the total force acting on the blade will not be affected because when the airspeed of the blade, aerodynamic lift, and inertia are considered we find that the total force remains constant. Individual blades will oscillate up and down about their flapping hinges (or gimbal) like a pendulum, and with a frequency which is equal to the number of revolutions per minute, the oscillations being heavily damped aerodynamically.

CONTROLLING CYCLIC PITCH

The Swash-plate System

When discussing collective-pitch changes, we noted how a rod attached to the blade can change the pitch of the blade by an up and down motion. If we trace the continuation of the rod in Fig. 39 we arrive at the more common system for moving it up and down once per revolution, thereby giving a cyclic-pitch change to the blade. It is called the swash plate.

The swash plate (or azimuth star) is divided into upper and

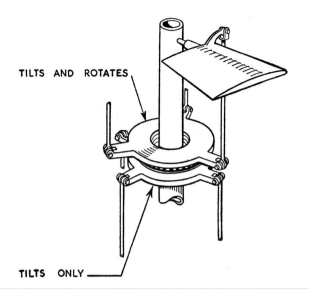

TILTS AND ROTATES

TILTS ONLY

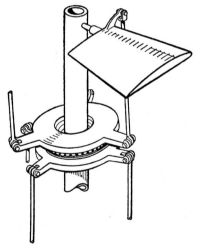

FIG. 39. THE SWASH-PLATE SYSTEM FOR CHANGING CYCLIC PITCH

lower sections with a bearing between the two. The upper section can tilt in any direction and it also rotates at the same speed as the rotor, as do all the rods and appendages above it. The lower section can only tilt, and it is from this lower plate (or *fixed star*) that control rods lead off through the usual type of control transmission to the pilot's cockpit, where is found the cyclic-pitch stick.

In order to tilt the rotor disc in any required direction for translational flight or any other manoeuvre, the swash plate must be tilted. The resulting up and down movement of the push-pull rods attached to the upper section (or *rotating star*) of the swash plate is transferred to the blades in the form of cyclic-pitch changes as the blades move round.

The rods which alter the cyclic pitch of the blades also control the mean collective pitch. This is done by making the whole of the swash plate move up and down bodily, or by arranging for part of the rotor hub or control linkage system to move up or down as required.

The Aileron System

As described in Chapter II, the rotor blades are designed to be torsionally flexible when this system is used, pitch-change bearings not being fitted. By changing the pitch of an aileron, tab, or servo flap, which is fitted on the trailing edge near the tip, the blade can be twisted and a change of pitch effected.

Alternatively, the aileron can be large in proportion to the rest of the blade, which is torsionally stiff and really serves as a mounting for the aileron. A change of aileron angle is similar to a change of pitch of a normal blade.

The Spider System

To the leading edges of the blades are connected the arms of a "spider". This is connected to the cyclic-pitch control axle which can be tilted about a central universal joint by operation of the stick in the cockpit. When the spider is tilted, the spider arm which is lowest will give a minimum pitch to its blade, while a maximum pitch is given to the position diametrically opposite. A cyclic-pitch change is thus effectively given to the blades. The control of collective pitch is merely a matter of raising or lowering the whole spider (Fig. 40).

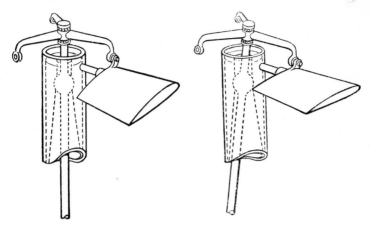

FIG. 40. THE SPIDER SYSTEM FOR CHANGING CYCLIC PITCH

THE PILOT'S CONTROL

The pilot's control for tilting the rotor, and thus obtaining translational motion in any direction, is the stick, or cyclic-pitch stick (also called the *azimuth* control or stick, or control column). The stick can be moved fore and aft and sideways or any combination of the two (Fig. 41) and the rotor will be tilted in the direction it is moved (obviously the rotor must be rotating for this to happen). When the stick is pushed forward, the helicopter will move forward, or, if already doing so, will accelerate. Similarly, if the stick is moved backwards or sideways the helicopter will proceed in these directions.

The stick works in a natural sense, and the degree of tilt of the rotor in relationship to the drive shaft depends mainly on the degree of stick movement.

Translational Flight in Tandem System

The method of obtaining translational flight in a tandem-rotored helicopter is worth noting.

In this type of helicopter there are two possible methods of moving forwards. The first method is to incline the whole of the helicopter by giving a differential change of collective pitch to the rotors (Fig. 42A). The second method is to give a forward tilt to both rotors individually (Fig. 42B).

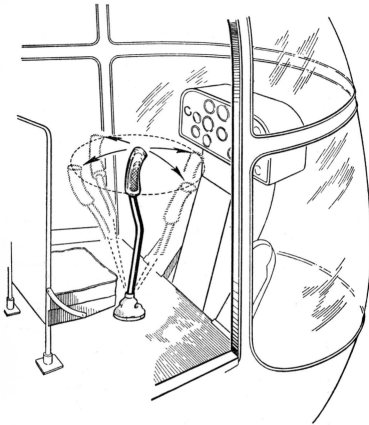

FIG. 41. THE STICK WHICH CONTROLS THE TILT OF THE ROTOR DISC

In practice, moving forward is carried out by a combination of the two methods, there being a trimming device to control the collective pitch of the rotors separately. Stated briefly, for normal manoeuvres the stick will apply cyclic-pitch changes to both rotors and, if a large stick movement is made, will also apply a differential change of collective pitch to each rotor.

Loss of Lift with Stick Movement

In any helicopter a change of stick position will often necessitate an alteration of power. For example, when the

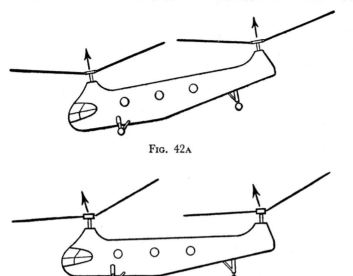

FIG. 42A

FIG. 42B

lift vector is tilted for forward flight, the vertical component
becomes less than it was during hovering flight (Fig. 43).

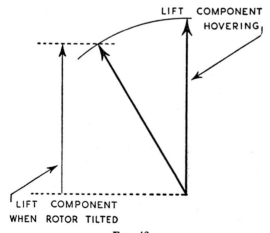

FIG. 43

Thus in the initial stages of translational flight the helicopter will lose height unless the pilot increases the thrust from the rotor. This he does by increasing collective pitch whilst keeping the r.p.m. constant.

Limiting Speed

Before finishing this chapter on translational flight it must be pointed out that there is a theoretical limit to the top speed of the true helicopter. The maximum speed is governed by—
1. The stalling of the retreating blade. (*Note*. A stall is said to have occurred when the angle of attack has increased so much that the streamline flow over the top of the aerofoil breaks down and becomes turbulent.)

When a helicopter is in forward flight part of the inner (root) section of the retreating blade is rotating in an aft direction at a speed which is lower than the forward speed of the aircraft. Air is therefore passing over the inner section of the blade in a reverse direction and there is a complete loss of lift (*note :* not a stall) at the root which will spread outwards along the retreating blade as the helicopter speed increases. Accordingly, all the necessary lift on the retreating blade must be produced by the tip.

In order to fly at high speed, collective pitch must be increased to obtain the necessary thrust, and in order to increase the horizontal component of thrust and to counteract dissymmetry of lift (see page 75) the retreating blade must be given a large angle of attack. The limiting speed of the helicopter is reached when the angle of attack becomes so great that the tip, which is now the only effective part of the blade, stalls. A marked vibration is then felt in the fuselage.

In order to delay the stall and increase the top speed of the aircraft, small fixed wings are sometimes fitted to the fuselage. They contribute some lift and therefore tend to unload the rotor. Level flight can then be maintained with less pitch than would normally be required.

2. The fact that, as the helicopter speed increases, the advancing blade will reach a high forward speed at which normal problems of aerofoils flying at or near airspeed Mach 1 (the speed of sound) will be met.

CHAPTER IV

MOVEMENT ABOUT THE NORMAL AXIS AND THE EFFECT OF THE TAIL ROTOR

THE normal axis of an aircraft is a straight line which passes vertically through the centre of gravity when the aircraft is in the rigging position.

TORQUE BALANCE AND DIRECTIONAL CONTROL

Now "to every action there is an equal and opposite reaction" (Newton's Third Law), so in a helicopter, when the engine

FIG. 44. TORQUE REACTION

rotates the main rotor, there is a tendency for the fuselage to be turned in the opposite direction. This is called *torque* reaction (Fig. 44).

The same thing is found in the propeller-driven aeroplane, where the tendency is for the fuselage to be rotated in the rolling plane in the opposite direction to the propeller.

Balancing Torque

Some means must be used to prevent the helicopter fuselage being turned. One of the most common ways of balancing torque is by use of a tail rotor, which by exerting a side thrust on a tail arm can be made to balance the torque and prevent the fuselage turning (Fig. 45). Note that, according to which side of the tail it is mounted and the direction of its thrust when balancing torque, the tail rotor will be either a "pusher" or a "puller".

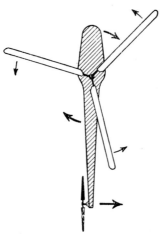

FIG. 45. BALANCING TORQUE BY MEANS OF A TAIL ROTOR

THE TAIL ROTOR. The tail rotor is driven by a take-off drive from the main-rotor gear-box and will always rotate when the main rotor is rotating. Rudder control is therefore always available in engine-off flight (in engine-off flight a free wheel fitted between the engine and gear-box automatically disconnects the engine from the rotors). The pilot can alter the collective pitch of the tail-rotor blades by using his rudder pedals. He cannot, however, control the r.p.m. of the tail rotor separately from the main rotor, and there is no mechanical cyclic-pitch change of the tail-rotor blades.

Hovering Turns

In the hovering condition, if the pilot wishes to turn the aircraft to the right (Fig. 46) he pushes on the right rudder pedal. If we assume that the main-rotor blades rotate anti-clockwise when viewed from above, then the pitch of the tail-rotor blades, and therefore the thrust of the tail rotor, will be decreased and the fuselage will be turned by the difference between tail-rotor thrust and main-rotor torque (unless the pedal is pushed to the limit, in which case the blades go into negative pitch and create a thrust in the same direction as the main-rotor torque). On applying this right rudder, tail-rotor

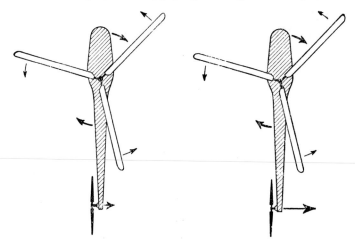

FIG. 46. TURNING RIGHT AND TURNING LEFT

thrust is reduced. The tail rotor then requires less power and the surplus will be absorbed by the main rotor. The r.p.m. of the main rotor will then rise, and unless the throttle is closed slightly the helicopter will tend to climb.

If the pilot applies left rudder, the tail-rotor thrust, which is used to balance the torque, is increased and the tail rotor will pull (or push, depending on which side of the fuselage the tail rotor is situated) the tail round to the right. Since the tail rotor needs extra power to do this, the normal r.p.m. of the main rotor will be reduced, and the helicopter will sink unless the pilot opens the throttle slightly.

Pitch-change Mechanism

To be able to change pitch, the tail-rotor blades must be free to swivel about their pitch-change axes. By attaching a rod to the leading or trailing edge of each blade the pitch may be increased or decreased by an inward or outward movement of the rod, in a similar way to the method used in main-rotor blades.

The three rods (assuming a three-bladed rotor) and the three-pointed star at the centre form a spider, the centre shaft

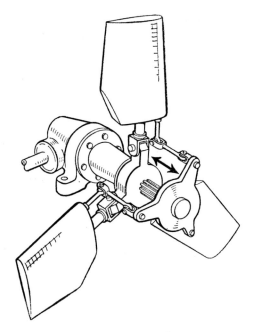

FIG. 47. BY MOVING IN OR OUT, THE SPIDER CONTROLS THE
PITCH CHANGES OF THE TAIL-ROTOR BLADES

of which goes through the centre axis of the tail rotor. This spider differs from the one mentioned earlier in connexion with the cyclic-pitch changes of the main rotor in that it does not tilt about a universal joint.

A typical tail-rotor system is shown in Fig. 47, the movement of the spider being controlled by a screw jack (not shown) which is rotated by cables on a pulley, the cables leading to the rudder pedals.

Other Systems for Maintaining Directional Control

Apart from the tail-rotor method, other systems may be used for balancing torque and giving directional control, and these are listed below.

1. IN SINGLE-ROTOR HELICOPTERS

(a) A tail propeller with its axis pointing aft can be used. Controllable rudders mounted in the slipstream deflect the air, thus providing a reaction which will give directional control.

(b) Instead of a tail rotor, a tail jet is used. The jet points to the side and by controlling its thrust directional control is given. In some designs the jet can be turned until it is pointing aft; it then provides propulsion to assist in high-speed flight, fins being used to balance the torque at high forward speed.

(c) With torqueless rotors (i.e. where the blades are rotated by jet reaction or other means on or near the tips) an adjustable aerofoil can be mounted on the tail below the main rotor. When hovering, the downwash from the rotor acting on the aerofoil will enable the pilot to have rudder control, and in fast forward flight the slipstream will do the same thing.

(d) In the gyrodyne principle, the tail rotor is replaced by a side propeller mounted on a short arm. The propeller balances the torque and also contributes to forward speed. Since the propeller is mounted on a short arm, however, it absorbs a large percentage of the available power and vertical performance tends to be reduced.

2. IN TWIN-ROTOR HELICOPTERS

(a) In the co-axial contra-rotating system the torques cancel each other out. Directional control is achieved by differential collective-pitch changes of the rotors, thereby creating a change of torque which will turn the fuselage.

(b) In the side-by-side twin-rotor system with the rotors either separate or intermeshing, the torques can be made to cancel out. Directional control can be achieved by tilting the rotors fore and aft in opposite directions to each other.

(c) In the tandem system with either separate or overlapping rotors the torques can be made to cancel out. Directional control is achieved by tilting the rotors laterally in opposite directions to each other.

3. IN MULTI-ROTOR HELICOPTERS

(a) Torques can be made to cancel out, and directional control can be achieved by tilting two of the rotors in opposite directions to each other.

FURTHER EFFECTS OF THE TAIL ROTOR

We have seen how the tail rotor prevents torque from turning the fuselage. Let us look at this in a slightly different way.

Couples and Moments

A couple is a pair of equal and opposite parallel forces which tend to produce rotation. It is a couple (torque) which

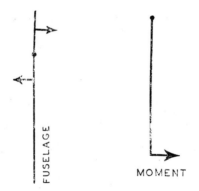

FIG. 48. A COUPLE IS APPLIED TO THE FUSELAGE BY TORQUE, WHICH WE TRY TO BALANCE WITH A MOMENT

is tending to make the fuselage of the helicopter turn when power is supplied to the main rotor (Fig. 48).

A moment of a force about a given point is the product of the force and the perpendicular distance between the given point and the line of action of the force. In a helicopter we are trying to balance a couple (torque) with a moment (tail-rotor thrust × the arm). It is not possible to achieve equilibrium in this way, for although the moment will stop the rotational effect of the couple, it will give rise to a resultant translational force and our helicopter will tend to drift sideways (Fig. 49).

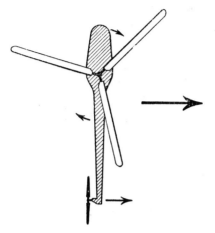

Fig. 49. The Tail Rotor tends to make the Helicopter Drift Sideways

Preventing Drift

This tendency is corrected by a design feature in which, with the stick central in the cockpit, the main rotor has a slight tilt to one side. This can be achieved either by the rigging of the cyclic-pitch system or by tilting the drive shaft slightly (Fig. 50).

The tendency to drift will vary according to how much power is being transmitted to the rotors. Variations from the average figure are dealt with by the pilot who places the stick to right or left as the case may be. Thus in a power-off descent the stick would be, say, to the right, while in the hovering condition, where much power is used, the stick would be to the left.

For convenience, the modern practice is so to design the control linkage that the rotor disc will tilt when collective pitch is applied, the stick position not being affected. This can be done only approximately, but it means that on the whole a change of power does not necessitate a change of stick position.

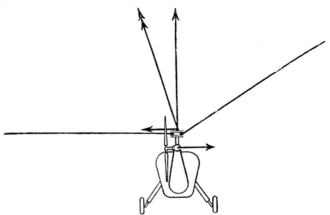

FIG. 50. DRIFT IS PREVENTED BY TILTING THE MAIN ROTOR
IN THE OPPOSITE DIRECTION

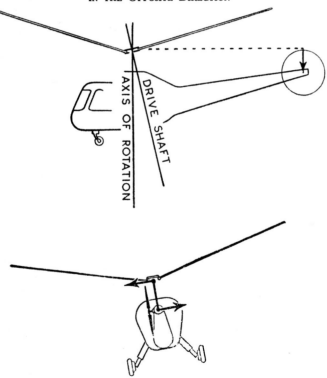

FIG. 51. THE TAIL ROTOR CAN CAUSE A ROLLING COUPLE

54

Influence on Hovering Attitude

A further effect of the tail rotor is its influence on the hovering attitude. It may be noticed in certain helicopters that hovering and landings are carried out with the fuselage tilted laterally and that the, say, left wheel always touches down first.

This situation will occur in a helicopter when the tail rotor is considerably lower than a line which is normal to the axis of rotation and which passes through the main-rotor hub. A rolling couple is therefore created (Fig. 51). The magnitude of the couple is dependent on the tail-rotor thrust and the vertical distance between the tail-rotor hub and the main-rotor hub.

It may be wondered why the fuselage does not tend to roll as a result of this couple, but clearly when the fuselage takes up a tilted attitude the centre of gravity is offset, thus producing, with rotor lift, a balancing couple.

CHAPTER V

MORE ABOUT THE MAIN ROTOR

It will be noticed that, when the helicopter is hovering, instead of the rotor blades sweeping out a flat circular area,

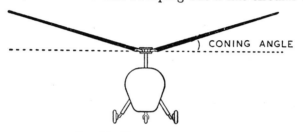

FIG. 52. THE CONING ANGLE

they sweep out the shape of a shallow cone. The angle between a blade and a plane passing through the rotor hub is referred to as the *coning angle* (Fig. 52). The plane is generally horizontal when the helicopter is in the rigging position.

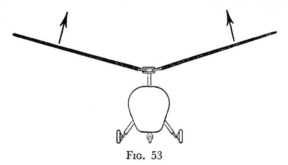

FIG. 53

The blades are caused to move upwards about their hinges by the lift which they generate during rotation (Fig. 53). There are three things which prevent the blades riding right up and assuming an almost vertical position—

1. Centrifugal force.

2. Gravity acting on the blades.

3. Rigidity (this applies only to rotors which are rigid or semi-rigid).

By far the most important of these is centrifugal force (Fig. 54). With lift and centrifugal force acting on it, a blade will

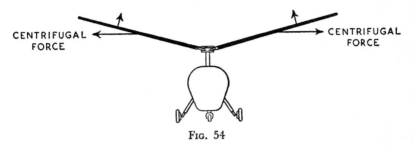

CENTRIFUGAL FORCE ← → CENTRIFUGAL FORCE

FIG. 54

take up a position which is roughly the resultant of these two forces.

We can now see that it is very important for the pilot to maintain a certain minimum rotor speed. If the r.p.m. becomes

FIG. 55. THE RESULT OF LOW ROTOR R.P.M.

too low, centrifugal force will become less and the blades will ride higher (Fig. 55). With the loss of effective disc area the helicopter will sink, and the upward flow of air through the rotor will assist in lifting the blades up to some point where it may be no longer possible to bring them down again.

Over-pitching

In connexion with the last paragraph, the pilot error of *over-pitching* should be noted.

When the rotor blades are over-pitched it means that their angle of attack is so great, and the drag so large, that the engine is not powerful enough to continue to drive them round, and the rotor will quickly slow down. The correction is to reduce pitch, and this action must be taken early or the helicopter will sink rapidly.

How the Blades Lift the Helicopter

As we have seen, when a helicopter is flying the rotor blades

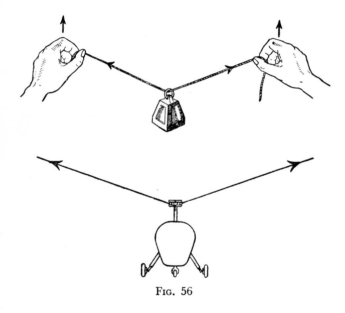

FIG. 56

take up a position which is roughly the resultant of blade lift and centrifugal force. This resultant will have a vertical component of lift, and it is this component which is tending to lift the helicopter. Just as an object can be lifted by a piece of string, so the helicopter is lifted (Fig. 56).

Translational Lift

A helicopter needs much more power for a vertical climb than it does for the same rate of climb with forward speed.

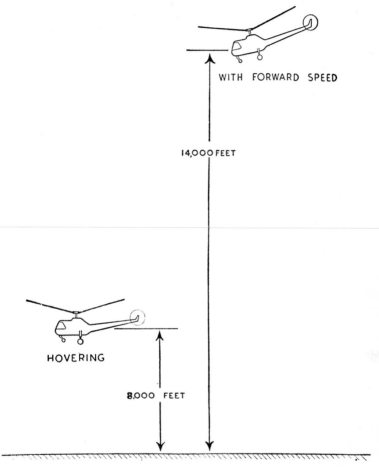

WITH FORWARD SPEED

14,000 FEET

HOVERING

8,000 FEET

FIG. 57. THE EFFECT OF TRANSLATIONAL LIFT ON THE CEILING OF A HELICOPTER

Similarly, its hovering ceiling is much lower than its ceiling with forward speed (Fig. 57). The reason for this gain in operating efficiency in translational flight can be simply explained if we realize that a rotor can gain the same lift by imparting a large acceleration to a small mass of air, as it can by imparting a small acceleration to a large mass of air. In the hovering case, where a large acceleration is given to a small mass of air, some loss of efficiency is experienced because the air which is approaching the rotor has been drawn towards it for some time and so has already gained some speed. In forward flight, however, the rotor enters a large mass of air which has not been "warned" of its approach, and the comparatively small acceleration given to the air enables the rotor to gain lift much more efficiently in this condition.

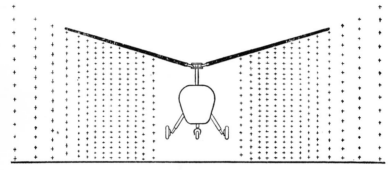

FIG. 58. THE GROUND CUSHION. EXTRA LIFT IS OBTAINED WHEN THE HELICOPTER IS HOVERING NEAR THE GROUND

It should be noted that this gain in operating efficiency is offset, as speed is increased, by the increase in drag on the helicopter. The best climbing speed is usually in the region of 50 m.p.h.

Ground Cushion

A helicopter can gain extra lift in another way. This is from the ground cushion (or ground effect) which is only apparent when the helicopter is hovering near the ground or water (Fig. 58) and which is caused by the air pressure below the rotor becoming even greater owing to the interference with the downwash.

When the rotor disc is tilted at an angle to the ground, for example just prior to hovering after an approach, the effect is not apparent. The cushion can, however, build up suddenly when the rotor disc takes up a level attitude, and the helicopter will then have a tendency to "balloon".

The ground cushion is of great benefit when taking off with a heavy load or in low air density (i.e. from a mountain top) for it is then possible to hover, whereas without the ground

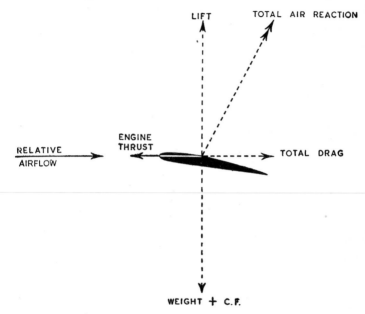

FIG. 59. FORCES ACTING ON A BLADE DURING STEADY FLIGHT

cushion taking off might be impossible. From the hover the helicopter can be moved forward gently, retaining the ground cushion beneath it until translational lift is gained for a forward-speed climb. The ground cushion is of practical value up to a rotor height above ground equivalent to the length of one rotor blade, although its influence can be measured at heights greater than this.

Effect of Gusts on R.P.M.

When a helicopter is in a steady condition of flight, a sudden up-gust will cause the r.p.m. to rise momentarily. Similarly, an increase in g in a sudden turn or pull-out will do the same.

This is because of the change in the direction of the airflow relative to the blades. Whereas the vector diagram was as shown in Fig. 59, the momentary condition is as given in

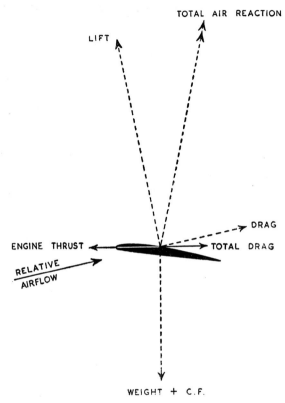

FIG. 60. FORCES ACTING ON A BLADE DURING AN UP-GUST

Fig. 60. Note how the total drag has decreased. Engine thrust on the blade remains the same, so the r.p.m. will increase. A down-gust will have the opposite effect and the r.p.m. will fall momentarily.

Definitions of Terms

The reader should now become acquainted with some terms of which the majority are peculiar to rotary-wing aircraft.

Disc Loading. Just as we have "wing loading" in fixed-wing aircraft, so we have *disc loading* and *blade loading* in helicopters. Disc loading (Fig. 61) is the ratio of the all-up weight to the rotor-disc area. Thus if we divide the all-up weight by the disc area, we have the disc loading in, say, pounds per square foot.

Blade Loading. Blade loading is the ratio of the all-up

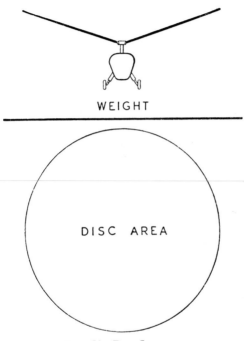

WEIGHT

DISC   AREA

Fig. 61. Disc Loading

weight to the total blade area (Fig. 62). Thus the all-up weight divided by the total blade area gives us the blade loading in, say, pounds per square foot.

Solidity. Another term used is *solidity* (a term also used in propeller theory), or the ratio of the blade area to the disc area. Thus blade area divided by the disc area gives us the figure for the solidity of a rotor (Fig. 63).

Power Loading. We talk about *power loading* in connexion with fixed- as well as rotary-wing aircraft, and it is the ratio

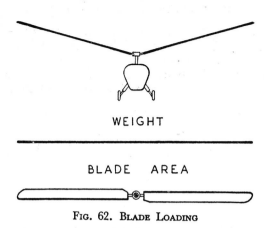

WEIGHT
_____

BLADE   AREA

FIG. 62. BLADE LOADING

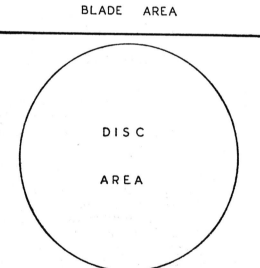

BLADE   AREA
_____

DISC

AREA

FIG. 63. SOLIDITY

of the all-up weight to the maximum horse power. Thus all-up weight divided by the horse power gives the power loading in, say, pounds per horse power (Fig. 64).

By reference to the figures for the above terms an expert can gain a good idea of the performance of the helicopter, not

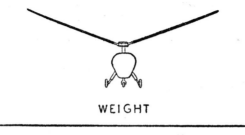

WEIGHT

HORSE POWER

FIG. 64. POWER LOADING

only in powered flight, but in power-off flight as well. The designer of a helicopter has many things to consider, and it is essential for him to keep the above quantities within certain limits because the all-round performance of his helicopter is dependent on them to a large extent.

Vibration

The disturbing thing about vibration in any aircraft is not so much the discomfort caused by it, as the fact that it can cause fatigue in metal, and a structural failure can result. In general, the vibrations which can be present in a helicopter may be divided into three groups: low frequency, medium frequency, and high frequency, and their source can often be located by comparison with the speed of rotation of various components.

For example, a low-frequency vibration is generally associated with the main rotor and may be a "one per rev." such as may be produced by one blade being out of track, etc., or a "three per rev." (assuming a three-bladed rotor) caused by blade stall, etc. A medium-frequency vibration might be caused by the tail rotor or the engine. A high-frequency vibration might have many sources. A hand-held vibrograph is a useful instrument for recording vibrations in flight. The results can then be interpreted on the ground, the faulty component located, and the trouble rectified.

Tracking

A common cause of vibration is an out-of-track rotor. Rotor blades are *in track* when the tip paths of all the blades coincide (Fig. 65). When out of track a rotor requires

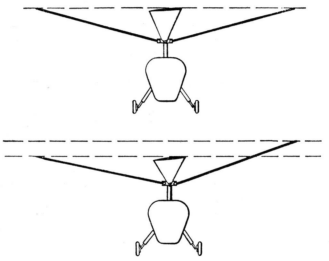

FIG. 65. ROTOR BLADES IN TRACK AND OUT OF TRACK

"tracking", which means finding out which blade or blades are riding high or low and applying the corrective action.

The more common methods used for tracking are—

1. THE FLAG METHOD. The blade tips are marked with different coloured chalks. The rotor is rotated at normal flying r.p.m. and as much pitch is applied to the blades as is possible without the aircraft becoming airborne (the aircraft can be ballasted or tied down if necessary). A canvas flag is brought towards the blades until the tips are touched and

chalk marks are left on the flag (Fig. 66). The chalk marks reveal the respective tip paths of the blades and show the amount of alteration required to bring them into track. The correction is made either by changing the blade pitch at the root in such a manner as to bring the blades back into a common tip-path plane, or by altering trim tabs (if fitted) on the blades.

2. THE BRUSH METHOD. The rotor is rotated as in the flag method and an oil-soaked brush with a long handle is brought towards the rotor tips from underneath (Fig. 67). The brush touches the lowermost blade(s), which, when stopped, is revealed by the oil mark. Correction of the offending blade(s) is then carried out by means appropriate to the type of helicopter.

3. THE MIRROR METHOD. Coloured mirrors ("cat's-eyes," etc.) are fitted under the blade tips. With the blades rotating, a lamp is shone at the tips and their relative positions can be seen. The blades are then adjusted by the means appropriate to the type of helicopter.

4. STROBOSCOPIC METHOD. An ultra-violet lamp is held by an operator in the cockpit and aimed at the underside of the rotor blade tips to which identifying material of different colours has been fastened. The lamp is triggered by an electro-magnetic pick-up fixed to the main rotor gear-box casing and flashes at a frequency equal to the number of blades per revolution of the rotor. Owing to the stroboscopic effect the relative positions of the blades can be more easily seen than in the mirror method. The blades are then adjusted by the appropriate means.

5. THE ELECTRONIC METHOD. The tip paths of the blades are ascertained electronically whilst airborne. Correction can be made by normal means, but the latest development allows the individual blade pitches to be altered *in flight*.

Counterweights

Sometimes rotor blades have external counterweights fitted to them. The purpose of these is to give the blades a pitch-increasing or pitch-decreasing moment which will balance any unwanted pitching moments of the blades caused by aero-dynamic or centrifugal forces.

It is a little difficult to see why centrifugal force tends to make a blade go into fine pitch, but if we think of a boy rotating a conker on a piece of string, we note that the conker

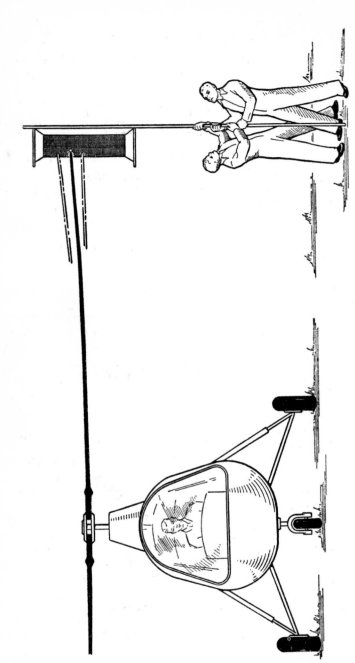

Fig. 66. The Flag Method of Tracking

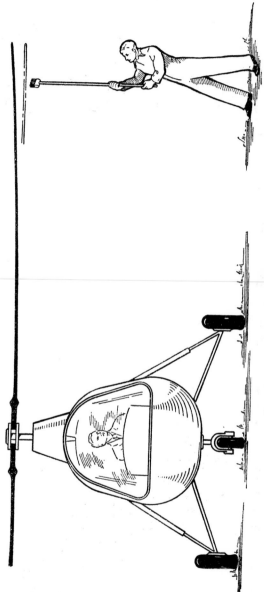

FIG. 67. THE BRUSH METHOD OF TRACKING

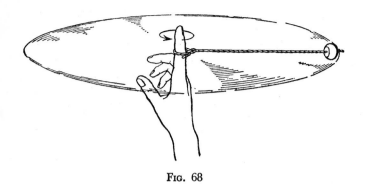

FIG. 68

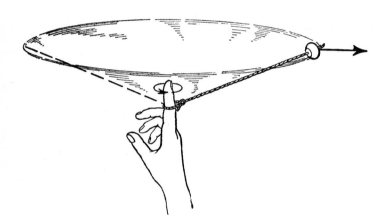

FIG. 69A

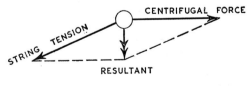

FIG. 69B

always wants to take up a position at right angles to the axis of rotation (Fig. 68).

If the conker is caused to rise, or the finger is lowered a little, then centrifugal force acting in the manner shown will tend to return it to the original position (Figs. 69A and 69B). Similarly, when a rotor is not in a coned position, any part of a rotor blade which is not on the plane formed by the pitch-change axis during rotation of the rotor will, apart from what other forces are trying to make it do, tend to move towards this plane, i.e. into fine pitch (Fig. 70).

In the same way, and whether the blades are coned or not, a weight fitted as shown would cause a pitch-increasing

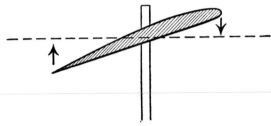

FIG. 70. CENTRIFUGAL FORCE TENDS TO MOVE
BLADES INTO FINE PITCH

moment when the rotor is rotating (Fig. 71). By careful choice of the weight and its position it can be made to balance any inconvenient blade pitching moments.

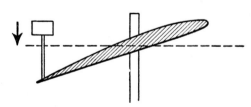

FIG. 71. A WEIGHT PLACED AS SHOWN WILL GIVE A
PITCH-INCREASING MOMENT TO A BLADE

Centre of Gravity

In single-rotor helicopters the centre of gravity lies approxi-mately on the normal axis. In an articulated rotor of the present small helicopters the permissible range of travel is about six inches. The permissible travel is considerably more in a helicopter which has a rotor with no freely-flapping blades (rigid rotor), or when the flapping hinges are mounted comparatively far out from the hub. The travel is also considerable in the tandem system where the aircraft can be trimmed by altering the differential collective pitch of the rotors (Fig. 72).

The lateral travel of the c.g. of a helicopter must be taken into consideration more than in a fixed-wing aircraft and care must be taken to ensure that unsymmetrical loads are not excessive. The normal theoretical method for finding the

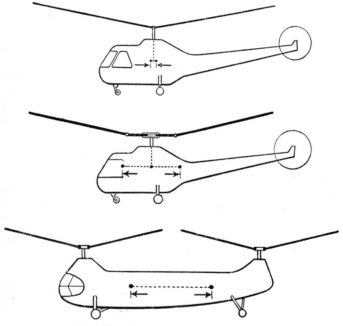

Fig. 72. Centre of Gravity Limits

centre of gravity position in fixed-wing aircraft can be used in a helicopter: this is, finding the algebraic sum of all the moments and dividing by the total weight.

CHAPTER VI

THE GYROPLANE AND SOME OF ITS LESSONS FOR THE HELICOPTER

As stated in Chapter I, a gyroplane (or autogyro) is "a rotor-craft that throughout its flight derives the whole or a substantial part of its lift from a freely-rotating rotor".

Juan de la Cierva invented the gyroplane and he gave his

FIG. 73. A GYROPLANE

aircraft the trade name of "Autogiro". It was from his aircraft that we obtained many of the ideas which went into the making of successful helicopters. In examining the flight of the gyroplane we find many features which help us to understand helicopter flight.

Let us now examine some of the differences between the gyroplane and the helicopter.

Differences in Appearance

GYROPLANE.   The gyroplane (Fig. 73) has a conventional propeller and a tail assembly, and may have wings.

HELICOPTER.   The pure helicopter has no propeller to pull it along, and the most common versions have a small rotor with a horizontal axis at the tail and at right angles to the longitudi-

73

nal axis of the fuselage. Other versions may have two or more main rotors and have no need for torque-compensating tail rotors.

Differences in Construction

GYROPLANE.   The gyroplane rotor is driven by the engine only when the aircraft is on the ground, either to start the rotor spinning or to use the facility of jump take-off, should this be fitted. During flight the engine drives the propeller only. The gyroplane pilot can control the tilt of the rotor, the power of the engine and possibly the rudder position. Wings may be fitted in order to unload the rotor in fast flight; other aero-dynamic surfaces are for trimming and stability purposes. If there is a jump-start facility a collective-pitch control may be fitted.

HELICOPTER.   The main rotor and tail rotor are driven by the engine(s). Some helicopters have wings. Sometimes a tail plane is fitted. The pilot can control the tilt of the rotor and its thrust. He can also control the thrust of the tail rotor.

Differences in Performance

GYROPLANE.   Forward airspeed is needed for take-off (see also *Jump-start Autogyro*, page 93). In calm air the gyroplane is unable to hover, climb vertically, fly backwards or fly sideways. Prior to its landing it must have forward speed, although the actual touchdown may be made vertically from a few feet up.

HELICOPTER.   The helicopter can hover, and it can fly in any direction (vertical or horizontal or combination of these) irrespective of its heading. It can rotate 360° under the main rotor while hovering or flying slowly.

Differences in the Attitude of the Rotor in Forward Flight

GYROPLANE.   The rotor is tilted backwards.

HELICOPTER.   The rotor is tilted forwards.

Differences in the Airflow through the Rotor in Powered Flight

GYROPLANE.   The airflow is up through the rotor (Fig. 74A).

HELICOPTER. The airflow is down through the rotor (Fig. 74B). An exception to this is when the helicopter is gliding (autorotating), in which case it virtually turns itself into a gyroplane as we shall see later.

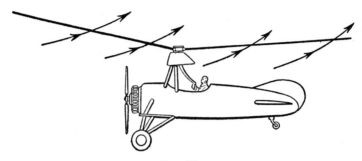

FIG. 74A

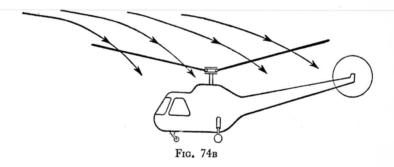

FIG. 74B

Dissymmetry of Lift

If one were to mount a simple rotor with rigid blades on to an aircraft and then taxi or try to fly forward into the wind, the aircraft would tend to roll. This is due to the fact that on one side of the rotor disc the blades would be advancing into the wind while the blades diametrically opposite would be retreating. The advancing blades would, therefore, be obtaining more airspeed and more lift than the retreating blades and the aircraft would roll towards the side of the retreating blades (Fig. 75).

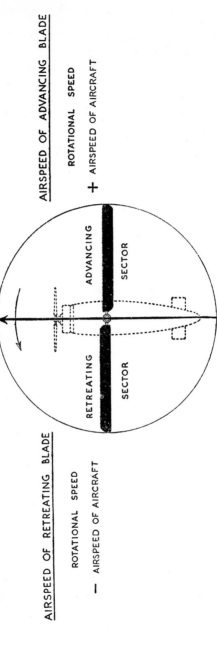

AIRSPEED OF ADVANCING BLADE

ROTATIONAL SPEED
+ AIRSPEED OF AIRCRAFT

ADVANCING

SECTOR

RETREATING

SECTOR

AIRSPEED OF RETREATING BLADE

ROTATIONAL SPEED
− AIRSPEED OF AIRCRAFT

FIG. 75. DISSYMMETRY OF LIFT IN TRANSLATIONAL FLIGHT

Corrections for Dissymmetry in Gyroplane and Helicopter

One can think of many ways of overcoming this problem in a gyroplane, although not all of them would be practical. For example, blades might be made telescopic so that the retreating blades could be given more effective area than the advancing blades. Or, the blades might be arranged to move at different speeds round the disc, the advancing blades moving slower than the retreating blades. Moving from the realms of fancy to more practical spheres we could think of arranging

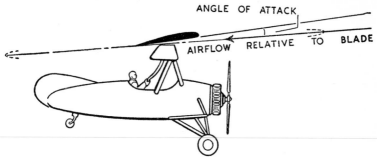

FIG. 76. WHEN A BLADE FLAPS UP, THE ANGLE
OF ATTACK IS REDUCED

main rotors in pairs with the rotors rotating in opposite directions, the rolling moments cancelling each other out.

It was Cierva who found a simple solution to the problem and he used it in his Autogiros, the earliest of which had no cyclic-pitch capability. He fitted hinges to his blades so that they were free to flap. To see how this achieves his purpose we must think of the airflow relative to the *blade* and the resulting angle of attack.

During rotation, when a blade becomes the advancing blade, it has increased airspeed and so has increased lift. It therefore rises about its flapping hinge. As soon as the blade flaps up, and while it is still moving upwards, movement of the air *relative to the blade* is changed from a horizontal one to a slightly downward one.

With a change in direction of the relative airflow, the angle of attack is altered and in this case is reduced (Fig. 76). When the angle of attack is reduced, lift is decreased, so the lift on the advancing blade will not, after all, be increased.

On reaching the forward position and just before moving into the opposite sector, the blade is in its highest flapped position.

When it becomes the retreating blade and is in the sector where its airspeed, and therefore its lift, would be reduced, the blade flaps down again about the flapping hinge.

The airflow relative to the blade now has an upward component so the angle of attack of the blade is increased (Fig. 77). At the rear of the rotor disc the blade finishes its downward travel and is ready to become the advancing blade again.

Thus by reducing the angle of attack of the blade when it is

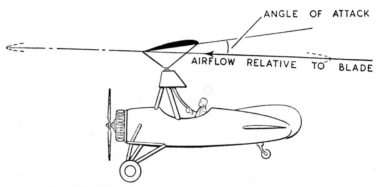

FIG. 77. WHEN A BLADE FLAPS DOWN, THE ANGLE OF ATTACK IS INCREASED

on the side of the disc where its airspeed is greater, and by increasing its angle of attack on the side of the disc where its airspeed is less, the lift is equalized on each side and the problem is overcome.

Note that a tendency of the aircraft to roll has been changed to a tendency of the aircraft to pitch longitudinally, for the rotor disc has been tilted backwards.

In the helicopter, the dissymmetry of lift problem is overcome in a slightly different way, for in order to move forwards, the helicopter rotor must be tilted forward. We can see that if the helicopter used the same method as the gyroplane to equalize lift, the flapping of the blades and the resulting backward inclination of the rotor disc would cause the helicopter to climb sharply as soon as any appreciable speed was reached.

The method used in the helicopter to correct dissymmetry of lift is one whereby the mechanical pitch setting of the advancing blade is reduced, while that of the retreating blade is increased. One's first impression might be that some form of supplementary control is required to cope with this. But it is carried out quite simply. It will be remembered that in order

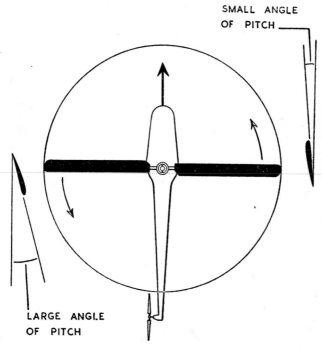

SMALL ANGLE
OF PITCH

LARGE ANGLE
OF PITCH

Fig. 78. Correcting Dissymmetry of Lift in a Helicopter

to move forward, the pilot pushes the stick forward, thereby giving the advancing blade a reduced pitch angle and the retreating blade an increased pitch angle. The resulting change in aerodynamic lift causes the blades to rise or fall on their hinges, thus inclining the disc.

Now, as the helicopter picks up speed, the blades will tend to flap just as they do in the gyroplane. The resulting tendency for the rotor to tilt backwards would, as mentioned, make the helicopter climb. As soon as he feels this, the pilot makes a control correction by pushing the stick *farther* forward. The advancing blade, which is the one tending to rise, is given a still greater reduction of pitch and therefore a little less lift. Similarly, the retreating blade is given a greater amount of lift (Fig. 78). If the pilot gives the right amount of forward stick movement, the rotor disc will remain in the required plane.

The pilot does not have to understand that this control movement is the result of the tendency of the advancing blade to flap up with forward speed. He is only interested in the fact that the nose of the helicopter starts to tilt up before he wants it to, and he applies the appropriate control correction without necessarily thinking of the reason for it.

In the helicopter main rotor, therefore, dissymmetry of lift is overcome mainly by cyclic-pitch changes. In the tail rotor the problem is overcome in a manner similar to that of the main rotor of a gyroplane—by flapping. Extra lift ("lift" in this case is a lateral force) on the advancing blades of a tail rotor, and reduced lift on the retreating blades, would, if uncorrected, cause a twisting force on the tail cone, but by allowing the blades to flap the lift may be equalized.

Autorotation

When helicopters were still something of a novelty in this country, many people assumed that if the engine should stop, the aircraft would crash. Had they understood that in the gyroplane the rotor blades are rotated solely by the air acting on them, they might have had some inkling as to what occurs in a helicopter when the engine fails.

When the rotor is driven solely by the action of the air on the blades, the rotor is said to be in *autorotation*, or to be *autorotating*. The definition of autorotation is: "the process of producing lift with freely-rotating aerofoils by means of the aerodynamic forces resulting from an upward flow of air".

In the gyroplane, the blades are autorotating all the time the machine is airborne. In the helicopter, the rotor is in autorotation only when the aircraft is descending with the blades at a low pitch angle.

Autorotation will be employed in the helicopter in one of the following circumstances: (*a*) the pilot wishes to descend at a faster rate than he could do with power applied to the rotor, (*b*) the pilot is practising an autorotative descent, (*c*) the engine has failed and the pilot is using the property of autorotation in order to make a safe engine-off landing, (*d*) the tail rotor has failed (this is extremely rare) and an auto-rotational descent must be carried out in order to avoid the effect of torque from the engine.

For a rotor to be driven round without an engine, air must be flowing upwards through it. In the gyroplane this can happen in all steady conditions of flight because the rotor is tilted backwards and is being dragged through the air by the tractor propeller. In the helicopter, there is no propeller to pull the aircraft along, and the flow of air in normal flight is caused by the main rotor which is driven by the engine. To obtain a flow of air without the engine, the aircraft must be descending. A free-wheel unit fitted between the engine and gear-box allows the rotor to rotate without being slowed down by a dead engine.

How Autorotation Works

Autorotation is usually likened to windmilling, and if a child were to ask how the blades move round without the

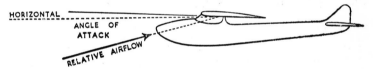

FIG. 79. DURING FLIGHT, A GLIDER WING CAN MAKE A
POSITIVE ANGLE WITH RESPECT TO THE HORIZON

engine, the simplest explanation is that the rotor is like a windmill and the air moves it round.

Despite the fact that we associate windmilling with a nega-tive pitch angle of the blades and autorotation with a positive one, the two have a basic similarity when relative wind and angles of attack are considered. It is outside the scope of this book to go too deeply into windmilling; instead we must discuss the question of what makes the blades go round.

The thing which puzzles us initially is the fact that it is difficult to see how a blade moves forward when it makes a positive angle with respect to the horizon. The analogy of the glider wing (Fig. 79) makes the position clearer.

During a normal glide, the wing makes a positive angle

with respect to the horizon. For a landing, the angle of attack is suddenly increased and the kinetic energy of the wing and fuselage is used momentarily to make the lift greater than the weight. If, however, during the descent the angle of attack is increased too much and for too long, the glider will slow down dangerously (Fig. 80).

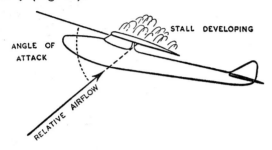

FIG. 80. A GLIDER WILL SLOW DOWN IF THE ANGLE OF ATTACK IS TOO GREAT

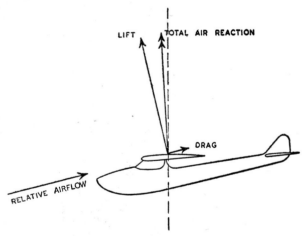

FIG. 81. THE GLIDER WILL ACCELERATE WHEN THE RESULTANT OF LIFT AND DRAG IS AHEAD OF THE PERPENDICULAR

The glider wing accelerates forward when the resultant of lift and drag (the total air reaction) is inclined ahead of the perpendicular (Fig. 81). There is then a forward component of the resultant tending to accelerate the wing.

Plate I. Juan de la Cierva, 1895–1936. (*Royal Aeronautical Society*). For extended captions to these photographs, see page 164

Plate II. Igor Sikorsky, 1889–1972. (*Flight International*)

Plate III. Rotor head of a large helicopter, the Westland Sea King. (*Westland Aircraft*)

Plate IV. One of the bifilar pendulum absorber arms mounted experimentally on rotor head. (*Westland Aircraft*)

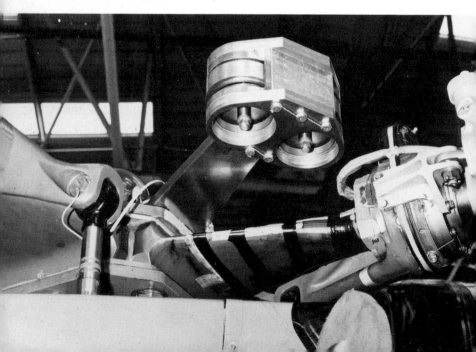

Plate V. The Sikorsky R.4. (*Flight*)

Plate VI. The S.51. (*Westland Aircraft*)

Plate VII. The Westland Widgeon. (*Westland Aircraft*)

Plate VIII. One version of the Westland Whirlwind. (*Westland Aircraft*)

Plate IX. The Westland Wessex Mark V. (*Westland Aircraft*)

Plate X. Westland-built Augusta-Bell 47G-3B-1. (*Westland Aircraft*)

Plate XI. Westland Belvedere. (*Westland Aircraft*)

Plate XII. Sikorsky S6.1N. (*Westland Aircraft*)

Plate XIII. Westland-built Sea King. (*Westland Aircraft*)

Plate XIV. The Lynx. (*Westland Aircraft*)

Plate XV. The Puma, or S.A.330. (*Westland Aircraft*)

Plate XVI. The Gazelle, or S.A.341. (*Westland Aircraft*)

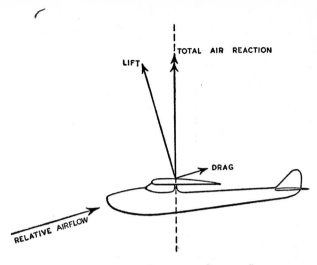

TOTAL AIR REACTION

LIFT

DRAG

RELATIVE AIRFLOW

FIG. 82. A GLIDER FLYING AT STEADY SPEED

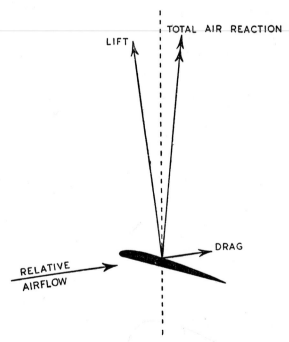

LIFT

TOTAL AIR REACTION

DRAG

RELATIVE AIRFLOW

FIG. 83. A ROTOR BLADE SLOWING DOWN

When the glider reaches a certain speed the forward component of lift is offset by the increase in drag. The resultant
then lies on the perpendicular, and since equilibrium is
now established the glider will carry on at a steady speed
(Fig. 82).

In the case of the helicopter rotor, everything can be simplified in our minds if we think of the rotor blades as wings
moving round on an axis. It is then simple to draw in vectors
under various flight conditions.

First, let us consider the case where the engine has just

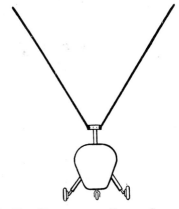

FIG. 84. THE RESULT OF A ROTOR SLOWING DOWN

failed and the pilot has not carried out the vital action of
instantly reducing collective pitch.

With a high angle of attack there is a great deal of drag.
The total air reaction vector, which is the resultant of the lift
and drag components (Fig. 83), will make a comparatively
large angle behind the perpendicular line and we can see that
the blade will slow down. With the loss of rotational speed,
centrifugal force, which is normally holding the blades out
against the lift force, will decrease and the blades will cone
right up (Fig. 84).

Secondly, the engine has just failed, but the pilot has
carried out the correct action and reduced pitch.

With the small angle of attack, drag is also small, and the
resultant of lift and drag is inclined well ahead of the perpendicular line (Fig. 85). The blade will accelerate and the

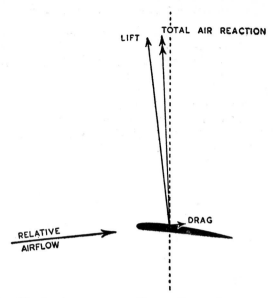

FIG. 85. AN AUTOROTATING ROTOR BLADE ACCELERATING

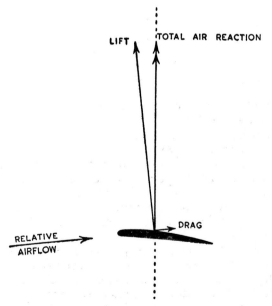

FIG. 86. AN AUTOROTATING ROTOR BLADE AT STEADY SPEED

85

r.p.m. will rise. The pilot likes this because there will be plenty of inertia in the blades. This inertia is equivalent to having power in the rotor and can be used just prior to touching down by increasing collective pitch, thereby cushioning the landing.

As the blade accelerates and the speed of rotation becomes greater, drag will increase and the total air reaction vector will not be inclined so far forward. When the vector is

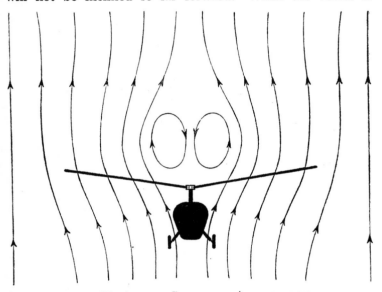

FIG. 87. AIRFLOW PATTERN IN AUTOROTATION

coincident with the perpendicular, the blade will achieve equilibrium and rotate at steady speed (Fig. 86).

During a descent in autorotation, the flow of air round the rotor will take up the pattern shown approximately in Fig. 87.

Increase in R.P.M. when Autorotating at Altitude

When a gyroplane or helicopter is descending at a high altitude, the rotor r.p.m. in autorotation will be more than they are lower down (unless, in the case of the helicopter, the collective pitch is increased slightly).

The aircraft will descend more quickly in less dense air.

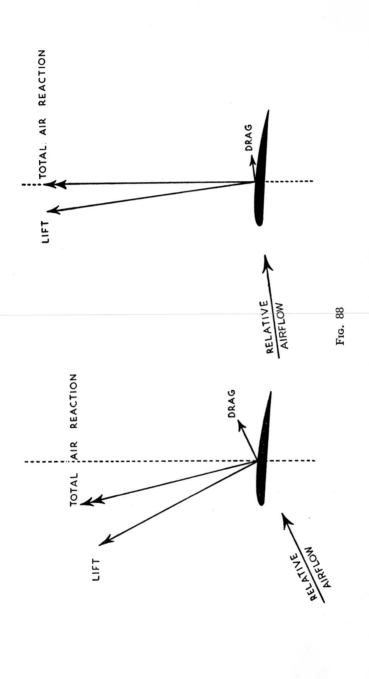

Fig. 88

This means that the angle of attack of the blades will be greater since the relative airflow has a greater upward component. It will be appreciated that the resultant will be inclined forward more than usual and the blades will accelerate until equilibrium is established (Fig. 88).

Dragging

Many rotorcraft have rotor blades which are free to drag. *Dragging*, or *leading and lagging*, is defined as: "an angular oscillation of a rotor blade in the plane of rotation about a substantially vertical axis" (Fig. 89). The axis is the drag hinge or part of the flexible root element.

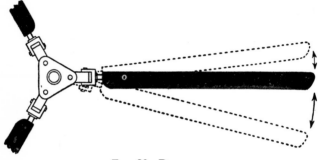

FIG. 89. DRAGGING

Drag hinges or flexible root elements are fitted because during flight each individual blade tends to move to and fro in the horizontal plane in relation to the hub or the other blades. If the blades were rigidly fixed, a bending moment would be set up, fatigue would be caused and the blade might break off. Alternatively the blades would have to be stressed for higher moments. By allowing the blades to move individually in the drag plane large bending moments are not permitted to occur.

Why Blades Tend to Move on their Drag Hinges

We must now answer the question of *why* the blades tend to move individually in the plane normal to the drive shaft. There are four reasons—

1. HOOKE'S JOINT EFFECT. The inclination of the rotor disc is obtained by the blades moving up and down about flapping

hinges during rotation. Thus although the rotor disc is inclined, the drive shaft remains fixed in the fuselage.

When the rotor disc is inclined at any angle other than that which is normal to the drive shaft, the blades tend to move on their drag hinges in order to maintain a constant speed.

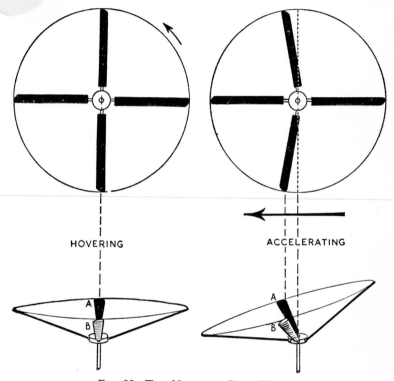

FIG. 90. THE NEED FOR DRAG HINGES

The explanation is simplified if we illustrate it with a four-bladed rotor (Fig. 90), the blades of which are at a fairly high coning angle.

In the case of the hovering helicopter, the blades are at 90° to each other with respect to the plane parallel to the plane of the hub.

When the rotor disc is tilted by blade flapping, the two athwartships blades, in order to maintain a constant velocity in the plane of rotation, must move on their drag hinges to the position shown. If drag hinges were not fitted, the blades would be forced to accelerate and decelerate with every revolution.

The situation occurring when the plane of the rotor disc and the drive shaft are not normal to each other is often referred to as the *Hooke's joint effect*. A Hooke's joint is a universal joint, but it is *not* a constant-velocity joint. Thus when the two shafts, with the joint in between, are not in line, although one shaft is rotating at constant speed the other one is rotating in a series of accelerations and decelerations.

It is possible to construct a helicopter which has neither the Hooke's joint effect nor the effect mentioned later in (3). In this type of design the rotor, which need have no flapping hinges, is mounted on a tilting hub with a *constant-velocity* joint. Instead of tilting the rotor disc by blade flapping, the hub is tilted—in this case by power-operated controls since there is a component of engine torque in the control system.

2. CORIOLIS EFFECTS. In a sudden up-gust or down-gust the coning angle of the blades will be suddenly and momentarily changed. This will cause a momentary increase or decrease in the rotational velocity of the rotor. If the sudden tendency of each blade to speed up or slow down was not allowed for, bending moments would result.

To see why a change in coning angle causes a change in rotor-blade speed, let us think of a boy rotating a conker on a piece of string. If he reduces the radius of rotation by looping his fingers and running his hand down the string, the speed of rotation will increase. This is due to the conservation of momentum. Similarly, when a rotor suddenly increases its coning angle, the distance of the c.g. of each blade from the axis of rotation is decreased and the r.p.m. will suddenly increase. The force causing the increase in r.p.m. is due to the inertia of the blade and is often referred to as the *Coriolis* force.

Note that the increase in r.p.m. due to the Coriolis force is separate from the increase in r.p.m. due to the change in direction of the airflow relative to the blade.

3. The third reason is that the Coriolis force can be present in translational flight owing to flapping of the blades with each revolution in order to tilt the rotor disc. For instance, in forward flight a blade is caused to flap up at the rear of the disc and the c.g. of the blade moves in towards the drive shaft.

The blade will therefore tend to move forward on its drag hinge.

Note. Inequality of movement of the blades about their drag hinges is one of the more usual causes of vibration.

4. PERIODIC DRAG CHANGES. For example, the retreating blade, on reaching the rear of the disc, will become the advancing blade and will meet an increased flow of air. The effect of the varying airflow on the blade is to cause oscillations of the blade in the plane of rotation, and bending at the root is relieved by allowing the blade to move about its drag hinge.

Rotor Blades which do not Drag

Some manufacturers favour a rotor with blades which are not permitted to drag. In these rotors, however, large bending moments will still exist in the dragging plane and the rotor must be designed to take care of them. The two-bladed rotor with blades which do not drag has some advantages over a rotor with three or more blades which do drag. Apart from the fact that it is impossible for the blades to be put in the incorrect relationship to one another owing to movement about the drag hinges, the two-bladed system has a lower weight and manufacturing problems are simplified. Maintenance is easier because individual flapping bearings are not required (the blades "see-saw" about a central gimbal), and without any dragging action drag dampers are not required.

The Need for Drag Dampers

Drag dampers are generally fitted between the rotor blades and part of the hub on all rotor systems in which dragging takes place. For damping, a hydraulic or friction system (Figs. 91A and 91B) is usually employed.

As the name implies, the function of a damper is to damp the dragging action. If the blades could oscillate in the drag plane in an unrestricted manner an unbalanced rotor system would result. If the dampers are not working properly, or if the manufacturers have chosen an incorrect damping rate, trouble might occur, especially in the form known as ground resonance.

Ground Resonance

Ground resonance manifests itself as a violent rocking of the aircraft on the ground. It can either build up slowly, the

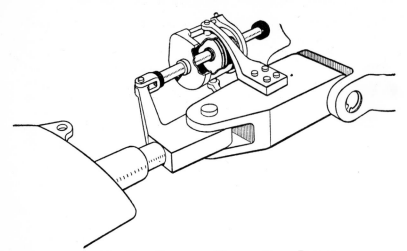

FIG. 91A. THE HYDRAULIC TYPE OF DRAG DAMPER

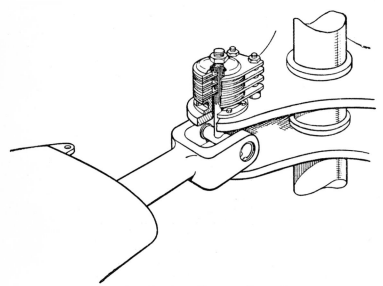

FIG. 91B. THE FRICTION TYPE OF DRAG DAMPER

oscillations gradually increasing in amplitude, or extremely rapidly. If uncorrected, the aircraft breaks up or rolls over.

The aircraft faults which might tend to cause ground resonance are faulty drag dampers, or incorrect pressures in the tyres or oleos. Piloting errors are generally those due to incorrect handling on the ground or when touching down; a forward speed landing on rough ground might also tend to cause it. In a proved helicopter, ground resonance is rare, in fact it is not always easy to reproduce it for training and demonstration purposes.

For ground resonance to occur, the main rotor blades must move in the drag plane and take up positions different from the normal 120° (assuming a three-bladed rotor) relationship (Fig. 92). The c.g. of the rotor is now off-set from the rotor centre. This unbalanced system is being rotated and causes oscillatory movements of the fuselage. When these movements are in phase with the natural lateral oscillations of the fuselage about the undercarriage or tyres then they will increase in amplitude and, if uncorrected, will reach the critical point where damage is caused. Longitudinal oscillations do not generally occur because the fore and aft pitching moments of the fuselage are too slow to be in phase with the rotor speed.

If action is taken early enough ground resonance can be prevented from developing to a critical point by applying power and taking off, or, if this is impossible, by shutting off the power and applying the rotor brake.

Jump-start Autogyro

Before leaving the subject of gyroplanes, mention must be made of the jump-start autogyro, which uses the *inertia take-off* in order to become airborne without a forward run. In the Cierva Jump-start Autogiro the drag hinge axes, instead of being mounted vertically, were set at an angle. This caused a decrease in blade pitch whenever a blade dragged back.

For taking off, a clutch was engaged and the rotor driven by the engine. With torque applied, the blades would drag back and move into fine pitch. When the clutch was disengaged, the blades would swing forward on their hinges and take up a positive pitch angle. The kinetic energy in the blades would last long enough to make the aircraft jump into the air, and, before sinking, translational lift could be gained for a forward-speed climb

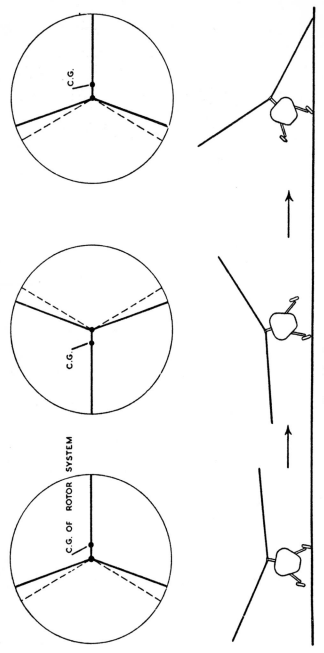

C.G. OF ROTOR SYSTEM

C.G.

C.G.

FIG. 92. GROUND RESONANCE

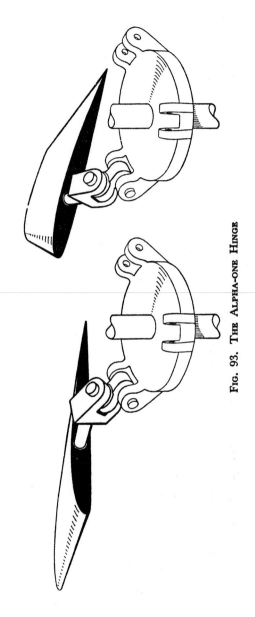

Fig. 93. The Alpha-one Hinge

A more positive control of collective pitch by means of a system similar to that used in helicopters was used in the Hafner gyroplane of the 1930s and is now being used in some modern autogyros.

Alpha-one Hinge

The drag hinge used in Cierva's Autogiros is known as the *alpha-one* hinge (Fig. 93), and according to its setting it can be either positive or negative. In the jump-start Autogiro the blades decrease their pitch angle as they drag back, so the hinges are negative ones. A positive version has been used in helicopters in order to create a constant-speed rotor. An application of engine power, causing the blades to drag back, instead of increasing the r.p.m. will merely increase the pitch of the rotor blades.

CHAPTER VII

STABILITY

THE term "stability" is used to describe the behaviour of an aircraft after it has been disturbed slightly from a trimmed condition.

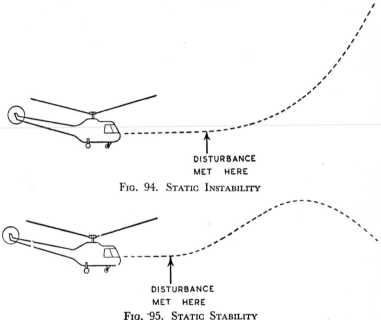

DISTURBANCE
MET HERE

FIG. 94. STATIC INSTABILITY

DISTURBANCE
MET HERE

FIG. 95. STATIC STABILITY

Static and Dynamic Stability

An aircraft is *statically unstable* if the displacement of the fuselage following a disturbance is in the same direction, i.e. if the nose is displaced upwards it will tend to move upwards even more (Fig. 94).

An aircraft is *statically stable* (Fig. 95) if, after a disturbance, its initial tendency is to return to its original position (whether or not the position is overshot).

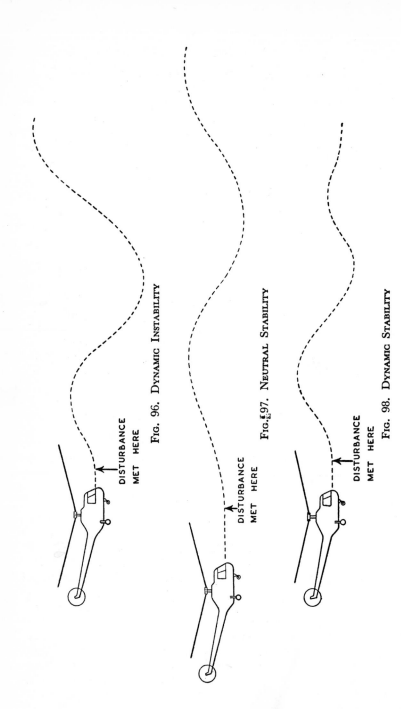

FIG. 96. DYNAMIC INSTABILITY

DISTURBANCE MET HERE

FIG. 97. NEUTRAL STABILITY

DISTURBANCE MET HERE

FIG. 98. DYNAMIC STABILITY

DISTURBANCE MET HERE

An aircraft is *dynamically unstable* (Fig. 96) if the oscillations following a disturbance are of increasing amplitude.

If the oscillations of an aircraft following a disturbance remain at the same amplitude, the dynamic stability of the aircraft is *neutral* (Fig. 97).

An aircraft is dynamically stable if the oscillations following a disturbance are of decreasing amplitude (Fig. 98).

Stick-fixed and Stick-free Conditions

There are two separate forms of the above stabilities to consider—

(*a*) *Stick-fixed* conditions: what happens if the pilot keeps the controls fixed.

(*b*) *Stick-free* conditions: what happens if the pilot leaves the controls alone.

Speaking very generally, helicopters at present are statically stable and dynamically unstable in the stick-fixed condition, and statically unstable in the stick-free condition. Longitudinal instability is much more marked than lateral instability owing to the high moment of inertia of the tail. Helicopters are usually fairly stable directionally (i.e. about the normal axis) in forward flight.

Fixed-wing aircraft tend to be dynamically stable. Hence one of the major differences in the piloting of a helicopter as opposed to an aeroplane in cruising flight is that the pilot must be continually making corrective movements to the controls. In the aeroplane the controls need hardly be touched once the aircraft has been trimmed.

Factors Affecting Helicopter Stability

There are three basic reasons why helicopters tend to be unstable dynamically. To follow these it must be remembered that translational flight is obtained by tilting the lift vector. Hence any change in the plane of the rotor disc will tend to cause the helicopter to accelerate in the direction of tilt.

1. The plane of the rotor disc will tend to follow any inclination of the fuselage.

With any tilt of the fuselage, and therefore of the rotor head, a cyclic-pitch change is applied to each rotor blade (in a similar manner to the tilting-hub control of the Autogiro).

The blade flapping movement that results from this will change the tilt of the disc and therefore of the lift vector. An acceleration will commence in the direction of tilt (Fig. 99).

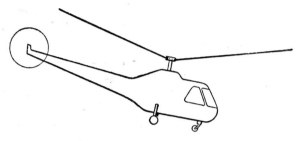

FIG. 99. IF THE NOSE MOVES DOWN, THE ROTOR WILL BE TILTED FORWARD AND ACCELERATION WILL COMMENCE

2. With any change of aircraft speed, dissymmetry of lift, unless corrected, will cause the blades to flap in such a manner that an increase in helicopter speed will tend to tilt the rotor disc backwards (this is often called "flap back") (Fig. 100),

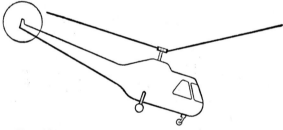

FIG. 100. AS SPEED INCREASES, THE ROTOR TENDS TO TILT BACKWARDS

while a decrease in helicopter speed will tend to tilt the rotor disc forwards.

(Paradoxically, it may be stated that a rotor tends to be stable with speed changes because of this tilting. When considered with (3), however, the overall effect on the helicopter is to produce a marked change in fuselage attitude.)

3. The centre of gravity of the helicopter is some distance below the rotor hub, hence a change in speed of the rotor system through the air will cause the momentum of the c.g. to

aggravate the tilt of the fuselage and therefore of the rotor disc.

The diagrams in Fig. 101 apply to an unstable arrangement.

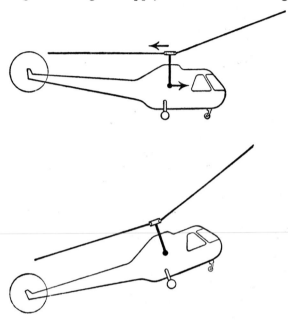

Fig. 101. THE HORIZONTAL COMPONENT OF ROTOR THRUST IS NOW REARWARDS. MOMENTUM OF FUSELAGE IS FORWARDS. THE AIRCRAFT TAKES A MARKED NOSE-UP ATTITUDE

Notice that the attitude of the helicopter in the instability sequence becomes more and more inclined. The helicopter will tend to repeat the motions, the oscillations becoming increasingly divergent.

Counteracting Instability

It is not proposed to go too deeply into the methods that have been used to make helicopters more stable. It will be sufficient to make brief mention of a few ideas which have been tried.

1. THE BELL SYSTEM. A weighted bar is attached below the rotor. The bar rotates with the rotor and, like a gyroscope,

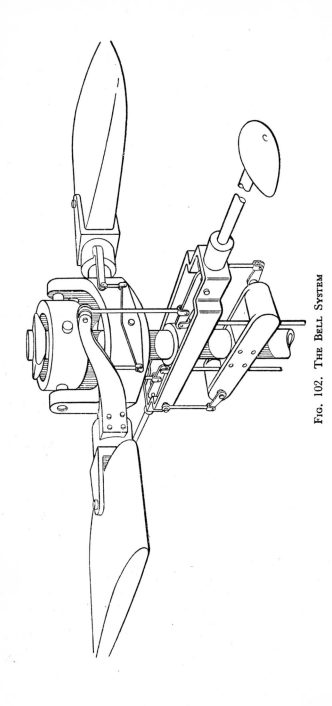

FIG. 102. THE BELL SYSTEM

tends to maintain a given plane. Control levers from the cyclic-pitch mechanism are linked to the bar (Fig. 102). Any tilt of the rotor disc tends to be corrected automatically by a system of mixing levers leading from the bar to the cyclic-pitch mechanism of the blades. Similarly a tilt of the fuselage is initially prevented from being transmitted to the rotor disc.

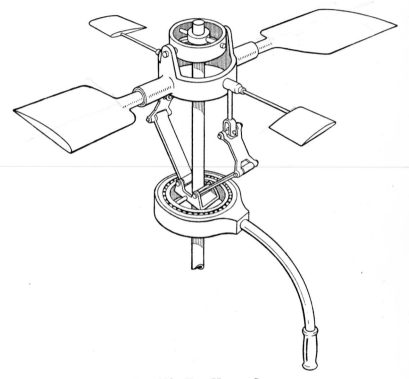

FIG. 103. THE HILLER SYSTEM

2. THE HILLER SYSTEM. Two "paddles" are mounted at right angles to the rotor blades and rotate with them (Fig. 103). Cyclic-pitch control is effected by changing the pitch angles of the paddles. The resulting flapping motion of the paddles will apply a cyclic-pitch change to the rotor blades and the disc will tilt in the usual way. If a rotor blade should flap up,

owing to a disturbance, the linkage to the paddles is such that a
change in pitch angle of the paddle, and its resulting flapping, will give the required pitch correction to the offending
blade.

3. THE DELTA-THREE HINGE. Instead of the flapping hinge
being mounted at right angles to the span of the blade, it is set

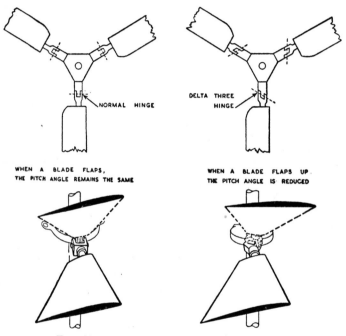

FIG. 104. NORMAL AND DELTA-THREE HINGES

at an angle (Fig. 104). Thus when a blade flaps up the pitch
angle of the blade is reduced. This tends to reduce the angle
of flap of the blade. The intention is that stability of the
helicopter will be assisted because dissymmetry of lift
will not cause such a large inclination of the disc due to
flapping.

The straightforward hinge as shown is not practical to use
in a helicopter because the pitch-change mechanism will be
affected. Instead, the control horn can be offset so that as a

blade flaps up, the leading edge will be pulled down by the horn and a *delta-three effect* will be given (Fig. 105).

The delta-three principle has also been used in attempts to create constant-speed rotors.

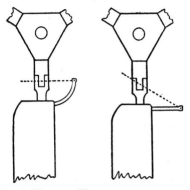

FIG. 105. A NORMAL HINGE; AND ONE IN WHICH
DELTA-THREE EFFECT CAN BE GIVEN BY OFF-
SETTING THE PITCH CONTROL HORN

4. Overshadowing all other methods of achieving stability is the automatic pilot, the development of which has gone ahead rapidly in recent years. When, in military helicopters, the automatic pilot is coupled to its own radar system a very sophisticated and precise method of automatic hovering control can be obtained.

CHAPTER VIII

PILOTING THE HELICOPTER

FOR those who love flying, the ability of the helicopter to hover and move in any direction from the hover with complete control gives a thrill and fascination that is not found in any other form of powered flight. From the passenger's viewpoint, the absence of speed when taking off or landing makes the helicopter feel safer than an aeroplane, and a more unrestricted view of the countryside from the cockpit, especially from the smaller models, can add a new enchantment to a familiar world.

Is the helicopter easy to fly? The answer is not straight-forward. Initially a student pilot may have more difficulty than someone learning to fly an aeroplane; but, when training is complete, helicopter handling is, perhaps, easier than it is in an aeroplane because of the simpler take-off and landing techniques, the flexible range of speed and the better view from the cockpit. On the other hand, since a helicopter is less stable than an aeroplane, the pilot may have to make more control movements than a fixed-wing pilot in order to maintain any flight condition. He will certainly be more tired after a few hours' flying in a helicopter without automatic stabilizing equipment than a fixed-wing pilot doing comparable work.

The initial difficulties in flying a helicopter are due mainly to the co-ordination required with the controls, the pendular swing of the fuselage under the rotor and the instability. Modern helicopters with improved stability characteristics, more sensitive controls and automatic r.p.m. control (in some gas turbine powered helicopters) are easier to fly than earlier models, but good control co-ordination still remains a skill that can be acquired only with practice.

Effects of Controls

The controls have been mentioned in earlier chapters, but a summary of their effects from the pilot's point of view is necessary to achieve understanding of the various flying manoeuvres.

In the hover, a displacement of the *cyclic-pitch stick*, or *stick* for short, but sometimes referred to as the *azimuth stick* or *control column*, tilts the rotor disc in the same direction and the helicopter tends to move in that direction. Thus a backward displacement of the stick results in a nose-up tendency followed by backwards flight, while a sideways displacement results in a sideways tilt and sideways flight. In normal cruising flight the stick is used 'much as is the control column in an aeroplane. The main difference being that if a rearward displacement were held for long the helicopter would, after climbing, lose airspeed and then tend to fly backwards.

The *collective-pitch lever*, called the *lever* (or sometimes the "*collective*") for short, has no exact counterpart in the aeroplane. In hovering flight, raising the lever tends to make the aircraft climb vertically and lowering it makes the aircraft descend. The primary effect of the lever is to control the power (measured in boost, or manifold pressure, in piston-engined aircraft; or in torque, measured in pounds feet, in gas turbine engined aircraft), and if constant rotor r.p.m. are maintained the power will vary with the lever position. The secondary effect of lever movement is a possible variation in r.p.m., but here much will depend upon the aircraft type, the qualities of the throttle cam and the manoeuvre being carried out. In gas turbine powered helicopters with automatic r.p.m. control a change of r.p.m. may be brought about by static droop.

The twist-grip *throttle* control, on the end of the collective-pitch lever, is primarily used to control the engine r.p.m. When moving the collective-pitch lever the throttle cam is a considerable aid in maintaining r.p.m., but the twist-grip throttle must often be used by the pilot as a fine adjustment, and he can still obtain any r.p.m. he desires over the normal engine r.p.m. range. The secondary effect of the throttle is of an alteration in power and a small change of twist-grip position can often cause a considerable change in boost. As mentioned before, in some gas turbine powered helicopters direct pilot control of the engine r.p.m. has been eliminated (see *automatic r.p.m. control*).

The *rudder pedals* are used in powered flight to balance torque, and to turn or tend to turn the helicopter in the yawing plane. As in an aeroplane, application of left rudder tends to yaw the nose of the aircraft to the left and vice versa.

In gliding flight (autorotation), rudder control is still available to maintain balanced flight or to turn in the yawing plane.

The initial complexity of control co-ordination will be appreciated when it is stated that the further effects of control movements are considerable. When one control is moved the other ones must generally be moved as well, especially in hovering manoeuvres. As an example of this let us consider the case of a helicopter that is about to move forward from the hover. The stick is eased forward. The aircraft starts to move forward, but sinks. Collective pitch is applied to maintain the height, the throttle position must then be altered to maintain the r.p.m. The change in torque means that the rudder pedal position must be altered in order to maintain the heading. The change in rudder pedal position affects the sideways drifting tendency and the r.p.m., and so on. When any forward speed builds up, the rotor disc will tend to flap back and more forward stick must be applied.

The control that causes the most difficulty is the throttle, especially as it does not move in a natural sense as do the other controls. As we have already seen, in some gas turbine helicopters the manual throttle is superseded by automatic r.p.m. control, thus making the pilot's task considerably easier. Monitoring of the r.p.m. is still important, however, in case of a failure of some part of the automatic system.

PILOTING TECHNIQUES AND MANOEUVRES

The following notes are intentionally brief and are not intended to be a do-it-yourself manual. They are written as a matter of interest to the reader and as a supplement to the more theoretical aspects found in the earlier chapters. For comprehensive coverage of helicopter piloting many hundreds or thousands of additional words would have to be written.

The helicopter assumed to be used in the exercises is a single-engined single rotor type with a torque balancing tail rotor. The r.p.m. are assumed to be controlled manually, but the normal maintenance of correct r.p.m. is not necessarily mentioned unless there is a definite reason for doing so. Unless otherwise stated the helicopter is assumed to be piston engined. Airmanship is not mentioned so it is emphasized now that the importance of the pilot keeping a good look out and obeying the various safety rules cannot be over-stressed.

The exercises are not in the order that a student pilot would be taught and some of the basic instructional exercises are omitted.

Taxi-ing

Normally a helicopter would be air taxied to any desired point on an airfield, but, assuming the aircraft has a wheeled undercarriage, ground taxi-ing is sometimes necessary to avoid disturbing other aircraft on the ground with the down-wash. To move forward, the r.p.m. are increased to the normal flying range with the throttle, the stick is eased forward and collective pitch increased with the lever as necessary to give sufficient thrust to move the aircraft. The aircraft is kept straight or turned with the rudder pedals. When there are cross-winds the stick is eased laterally into the wind to avoid any tendency to roll over. To stop, either the wheel brakes are applied or the stick is eased back with care, the collective-pitch lever being lowered on coming to a halt.

Taking off to the Hover

When heading into wind (although cross-wind or downwind take-offs can be carried out if necessary), the throttle is opened to obtain normal flying r.p.m. The collective-pitch lever is raised, the necessary rudder is applied to maintain the heading and the stick is used to keep the aircraft from pitching, rolling or moving in any direction when becoming airborne.

When taking off on sloping ground the technique is varied slightly in that the stick is held uphill. As the lever is raised, lifting the downhill part of the aircraft, the stick is eased pro-gressively back to the normal position until the aircraft is airborne at the normal hovering attitude.

Hovering

To an outside observer or to a passenger, hovering looks easy. The pilot is apparently doing little and the aircraft is virtually still. In fact the pilot is making constant small corrections with all the controls. He is maintaining position with the stick, keeping height (generally at up to five feet wheel clearance) with the collective-pitch lever, retaining the heading with the rudder pedals and correcting any change of r.p.m. with the throttle.

Vertical Movements from the Hover

Vertical movements from the hover are carried out by raising or lowering the collective-pitch lever as required. Secondary effects are considerable. Since the torque is being altered a change in rudder pedal position is necessary. This in its turn will affect the r.p.m. and the sideways drifting tendency of the helicopter.

Unless absolutely necessary, vertical climbs, slow speed flight and hovering should not be carried out between 10 ft and 400 ft in a single-engined helicopter. In this speed/height band an engine failure could be dangerous as proper autorotation could not be established for a controlled landing. Below ten feet there is sufficient inertia in the rotor for cushioning a landing in the event of engine failure.

Correcting Over-pitching

As we have seen in earlier chapters, over-pitching is a piloting error generally brought about when carrying out hovering manoeuvres, or when taking off, by using excessive collective pitch. In the over-pitched condition drag on the rotor blades becomes so great that even at full power the engine cannot maintain the normal rotor r.p.m. and the aircraft sinks. A pilot is naturally more prone to make the error when the aircraft is at maximum all-up weight or at high altitudes, or when it is a hot calm day. The tendency to over-pitch will also vary among different helicopter types according to the power available and clearly a pilot is more likely to over-pitch an under-powered helicopter.

True over-pitching occurs with the throttle fully open, the collective-pitch lever in a high position and the boost at its normal maximum or greater. To demonstrate the condition in aircraft with good power margins at sea level it is often necessary to simulate it by hovering at reduced r.p.m. and raising the collective-pitch lever high. This will cause the r.p.m. to fall and the helicopter to sink.

The correction for over-pitching is comparatively simple, provided it is carried out early, otherwise the aircraft may hit the ground heavily. Once over-pitching is recognized the collective-pitch lever must be lowered a few degrees while the throttle is held fully open. As soon as normal r.p.m. have been recovered hovering may be resumed.

Flying Sideways and Backwards: Air taxi-ing

The stick is eased in the direction it is required to move and is then used to control the ground speed at about five to ten knots. Height is controlled by the collective-pitch lever, the heading with the rudder pedals and the r.p.m. with the throttle. For air taxi-ing, the helicopter is generally turned out of wind, if the wind is not too strong, and flown forward to the position required.

Transitions from the Hover to the Hover

This is a form of longer distance air taxi-ing and as a co-ordination exercise for students it is excellent.

A transition in this case consists of a hover, a gradual acceleration forward into wind to about 50 kt airspeed and a gradual return to the hover again, *all at a fixed altitude of about 20 ft.* It should not be confused with a *quick stop* which is an advanced manoeuvre carried out more quickly and one in which the rotor is autorotating at one stage.

The first part of a transition is not too difficult as the technique is much like that for the initial part of a forward speed climb, where the aircraft is accelerating forward to gain speed, power being reduced, however, when the required airspeed is reached. It is the slowing down that requires careful attention. The easing back of the stick—and this should be a very small movement—must be accompanied, or even preceded by a downward movement of the collective-pitch lever. This in turn will call for a corresponding change of rudder pedal position to keep straight and a change of twist-grip throttle position in order to maintain the correct r.p.m. As translational lift is lost, power must again be increased with a corresponding requirement for balancing torque and maintaining r.p.m.

Turns on the Spot: also called Spot Turns or 360° Turns

These are simple to do in calm air, but in a wind it must be appreciated that relative to the air the helicopter will be alternately moving forwards, sideways, backwards, sideways and then forwards again while turning on its axis a few feet over a fixed spot on the ground. Also, the weathercock stability of the helicopter (caused by the tail) is such that the initial turn out of wind will be resisted and on passing the downwind position the rate of turn will tend to speed up. Again, due to the wind, a fair amount of rudder will be necessary to make and control the turn and this will have a considerable effect on the r.p.m.

Bearing these factors in mind, the turn is initiated and controlled with the rudder pedals, position is maintained with the stick, height is controlled with the collective-pitch lever and the r.p.m. are controlled with the throttle.

This exercise is useful for co-ordination practice and it will also enable the pilot to look round for other aircraft and obstructions.

Landing

The necessity for a good landing is good hovering. Having achieved a good hover the helicopter is lowered slowly on to the ground by use of the collective-pitch lever. After touchdown the lever is lowered fully and the engine then throttled back to an appropriate idling figure. Landing is not as easy as it sounds, for lowering the collective-pitch lever produces various secondary effects and the aircraft will tend to lose its position and heading.

Landings on sloping ground require a slightly different technique. After touching the ground with the uphill part of the undercarriage the stick must be eased progressively uphill as the aircraft is allowed to settle slowly on to the remainder of the undercarriage.

Recovery from Ground Resonance

Ground resonance is discussed in an earlier chapter and the deliberate introduction of it by his instructor is not normally necessary more than once during a pilot's training. It should be induced only if the type of aircraft being used for training is suitable for it.

When ground resonance has started the student must raise the collective-pitch lever smartly in order to get away from the ground. The alternative action of closing the throttle and applying the rotor brake should not be carried out in the case of deliberately induced ground resonance as the aircraft may break up before recovery is complete. This action should be used only in an emergency when it is impossible to take off.

Transition to the Climb from the Hover

The stick is eased forward and power is increased. When the aircraft has gained some forward speed the rotor disc will tend to "flap back" owing to dissymmetry of lift and this tendency must be prevented or corrected. As the aircraft accelerates, either level flight or a slight climb is maintained. When the best climbing airspeed (anything from 40 kt to 65 kt depending upon the type of helicopter) is reached the stick is eased back to maintain that speed (or, for safety, a slightly higher speed for the first few hundred feet). In some helicopters maximum permissible power may be used for the initial climb and at about 300 ft reduced to normal climbing power.

Continuous Climbs

During the climb, fore or aft displacement of the stick is used to control the airspeed, lateral level being controlled by lateral use of the stick. As soon as the proximity of the ground ceases to be important the collective-pitch lever is used to control the boost, rather than as a precise control for height as it is in hovering manoeuvres.

The difference between a zero airspeed climb and a climb with forward speed should be noted. Vertical climbs require, relatively, a great deal of power, whereas forward speed climbs can be carried out at the same rate with less power because of translational lift. Also, with forward speed the helicopter can zoom at any time so that a rapid rate of climb can be achieved momentarily.

Flying Straight and Level from the Climb

The airspeed is increased by easing the stick forward. As normal cruising speed is reached the r.p.m. and boost are reduced to the normal cruising power.

Straight and Level Flight

In straight and level flight the airspeed is controlled basically by the stick and the maintenance of altitude is controlled basically by the collective-pitch lever which, in its turn, is controlling the boost. Generally, use of these two controls has to be co-ordinated. To increase the airspeed, for example, the stick is eased forward and at the same time the lever is raised slightly to give more power. The lateral attitude of the aircraft is controlled by lateral use of the stick. The rudder pedals are used to balance the aircraft in the yawing plane so that there is no slip or skid (as shown by the slip indicator, or ball).

Recovery from Blade Stall

As we saw in an earlier chapter, blade stall occurs when at high forward airspeeds the angle of attack of the retreating blade is made so great that the streamline flow over the upper surface of the tip of the blade breaks down. Each blade will stall in turn when it is the retreating blade. The high angle of attack can also be increased beyond the critical angle and cause blade stall in manoeuvres such as a steep turn, or by up-gusts. Again, the airspeed at which blade stall commences will be reduced when the aircraft has a high all-up weight or when it is at high altitudes as a greater degree of collective pitch must be used in these conditions.

The pilot feels blade stall as a vibration equivalent to the number of blades in the rotor per revolution, i.e. in a three-bladed rotor there is a three per revolution vibration. The vibration can be fairly severe and a kicking in the controls may also be apparent.

When blade stall occurs one or more of the following actions should be carried out in accordance with the flight condition.

1. Reduce the Severity of the Manoeuvre

This is applicable if the blade stall occurs in steep turns, sharp pull outs at high speed, etc.

2. Reduce Collective Pitch

This is the corrective action that could be applied in the majority of cases, especially when flying fast in turbulent weather conditions. In helicopters that are prone to high speed stalling of the advancing blades (due to their reaching their critical Mach number) it may not be possible to know which of the two possible causes are producing the vibration. A slight reduction of r.p.m. may, therefore, be advisable at the same time as the collective-pitch lever is lowered.

3. Reduce Airspeed

The argument against an immediate reduction of airspeed in the case of blade stall at high cruising speeds is that the result of easing back the stick would be to increase the *g* and aggravate the stall symptoms. Therefore the reduction of airspeed should be done gradually and collective pitch should be reduced at the same time.

4. Increase Rotor R.P.M.

If higher rotor r.p.m. can be used with a lower collective pitch then the cruising speed at which blade stall will occur will be higher. In some aircraft the possibility of reaching critical Mach numbers with the advancing blades must be borne in mind when the r.p.m. are increased.

In pilot training, much depends upon the type of helicopter being used as to the manner in which blade stall is induced for demonstration purposes. With some aircraft the onset of blade stall may be experienced fairly frequently during routine exercises; in the other extreme, steep turns with high *g* effects at altitude may have to be carried out before blade stall can be experienced.

Turns in Cruising Flight

Turns are very similar to those carried out in aeroplanes. Banked turns are made but, unlike turns in those aeroplanes which fly at comparable airspeeds, little use is made of the rudder pedals and a balanced turn can often be made without pedal movement. The turn is initiated by easing the stick to port or starboard as required and then, as the aircraft banks, easing the stick back slightly to prevent the nose dropping and to assist in turning. Any tendency to slip or skid can be controlled with the rudder pedals. As the angle of bank increases, power may have to be increased to maintain the airspeed without loss of height.

A *steep turn* in a helicopter is generally made at an angle of 30° or more depending on the aircraft type.

Powered Descents

To enter a powered descent from the cruising condition the collective-pitch lever is lowered to a low power condition (but not low enough to enter autorotation) and, at the same time, the airspeed is reduced to a convenient figure (generally about the same as the best climbing speed) by easing back on the stick. The r.p.m. are reduced by a very small amount only, or not at all, depending upon the helicopter type. With the change in torque, a fair amount of rudder must be applied to keep straight and in balance.

Climbing and Descending Turns

These are banked turns carried out during climbs and descents. The turn is initiated by easing the stick to port or starboard as usual. In a descending turn an unusual feature, especially noticeable to aeroplane pilots, is the fact that the aircraft may be turning to *port* but that a considerable amount of *right* rudder is necessary to maintain balanced flight due to the low rotor torque.

Transition to the Hover from a Powered Descent

A powered descent is continued into wind at normal descent speed. When the helicopter is at about 100 ft above ground the airspeed is reduced gradually by easing back on the stick. Power is increased as necessary after the aircraft has lost some of its speed. The aircraft should have stopped descending and a zero ground speed attained at about 10 ft above ground. A normal landing can then be made if desired. Attempts by students to slow down rapidly or to do steep approaches complicate their control co-ordination problem and are best left until more skill has been gained.

Steep Approaches

Steep approaches are often necessary when approaching to land in small or restricted sites. A slow rate of descent should be made at a steep angle or even vertically and, depending on the wind speed, the I.A.S. will be low or even zero. Assuming that there is sufficient power available, there are two main problems during the approach: firstly, as the descent is steepened the pilot's view of the ground and obstructions may be cut off by parts of the fuselage; secondly, there is a possibility of entering the vortex ring condition.

The first problem can be alleviated by a thorough inspection of the site from the air before attempting an approach and then executing the type of approach most suitable for the situation; signals from the ground are also of assistance during the approach. The vortex ring problem is discussed in the following exercise.

Flight in, and Recovery from, the Vortex Ring Condition

The vortex ring condition can occur during a vertical descent through the air with power on, a rate of descent in excess of 300 ft per minute usually being necessary. It can also occur, although this is less common, in a condition where there are comparatively strong *g* effects at slow speed with considerable power applied and with the helicopter mushing through the disturbed air. The latter case is generally momentary, but may cause considerable buffeting coupled with a loss of lift. In the case of the vertical descent the effect can be prolonged and can result in a high rate of descent, vibration and partial loss of control, although the symptoms may vary considerably among different helicopter types. The condition is not dangerous unless carried out at low altitude as the rate of descent is high both during the condition and the recovery from it, so it should not be held deliberately below 600 ft. Steep or vertical approaches to small sites in calm air should be carried out at a low rate of descent in order to avoid the vortex ring condition.

The vortex ring condition is so named because of the airflow pattern round the rotor as shown in Chapter II. From the pilot's point of view it may be thought of more simply as the fact that the rotor is forcing air downwards and the aircraft is then sinking into this downward moving and disturbed air. It is not always easy to initiate the condition for demonstration purposes as sideways, forward or backward movement through the air could prevent it occurring.

When the condition is encountered in a vertical descent there are two ways of recovering from it—

1. Easing the stick forward and diving out.

2. Entering autorotation (placing the collective-pitch lever fully down) and diving out.

Entry into Autorotation

An entry into autorotation can be made in two ways—

1. It can be made very gently so that a passenger could hardly notice the change from level flight to gliding flight. This method is generally used when there is no emergency and the pilot is merely entering gliding flight for a fast descent.

To enter autorotation in this manner from cruising flight, the collective-pitch lever is lowered slowly, the r.p.m. being maintained with the throttle and rudder being applied to keep straight during the reduction of torque. Easing back on the stick at the same time will reduce the airspeed and also reduce the rate of descent initially. When the collective-pitch lever is on the bottom stop, or near it, the throttle is closed and the engine r.p.m. reduced to a convenient idling figure, the free-wheel operating to allow the disparity between normal engine and rotor r.p.m. and the tachometer needles "splitting" as shown in Fig. 20E.

2. In the case of an engine failure or a practice engine failure the action of the pilot must be immediate and the collective-pitch lever lowered instantly to the bottom stop. In a true engine failure the rotor r.p.m. will probably have dropped considerably before the pilot's action, depending on the flight conditions at the time, i.e. the fall in rotor r.p.m. would be considerable if the failure happened in a climb, but much less in a powered descent. Whereas a passenger might not notice an entry into autorotation in the slow type of entry, he would certainly notice it in this type of entry as the aircraft will drop very suddenly. If the engine failure happens in cruising flight, easing back on the stick as the lever is lowered will tend to lessen the drop of rotor r.p.m. and will also make the change to autorotation less abrupt.

Flight in Autorotation

Full directional control is available in autorotation so turns may be carried out. The rotor will autorotate in all possible conditions of flight provided the collective-pitch lever is kept down at or near the bottom stop, so the airspeed may be increased to the maximum or reduced to zero as desired and the aircraft can be flown backwards or sideslipped or rotated about the vertical axis during the descent.

A trained pilot will usually make most of his normal descents in autorotation, continuing with a powered approach at about 100 ft above ground.

Control of Rotor R.P.M. in Autorotation

Once autorotation has been established and provided the collective-pitch lever is kept on its lower stop, the rotor r.p.m. cannot fall to a dangerously low figure. The effect of an increase in *g*, low air density, high all-up weight or a high airspeed, however, might be to cause an unacceptable rise in rotor r.p.m. to the maximum limit. This can be avoided or corrected by raising the collective-pitch lever. It is either raised slightly and held in that position, as might be the case when in a steady descent at high altitude, or, it is momentarily raised, sometimes by quite large amounts, to prevent the rapid increase in r.p.m. that can occur during certain manoeuvres or when flying in disturbed air.

Controlling the Angle of Glide with the Airspeed

The glide path angle through the air will alter according to the airspeed used during the descent. A steep or vertical approach can be carried out at very low airspeeds. A flatter glide path can be achieved at higher airspeeds, up to a certain limit. Rotor r.p.m. also affect the glide path and when flying for range in autorotation the r.p.m. can be reduced by judicious use of the collective-pitch lever in order to further flatten the glide path.

Whatever airspeed is used, it must be reverted to the correct range of airspeeds for an engine-off landing, and the aircraft should be into wind, before the final phase of the approach is made. This is especially important if an initial vertical descent has been made as much height is quickly lost when the stick is eased forward to gain airspeed. Reversion to normal airspeeds can be delayed if necessary, however, in the case of an initial descent in the higher range of airspeeds.

Spot Autorotations

There is no merit in a pilot being able to do a good engine-off landing unless he can first position the aircraft on the approach to a suitable field. The manoeuvre in which a helicopter is autorotated down to a pre-selected position and then either landed or climbed away again at about 100 ft is called a *spot autorotation*.

In the previous exercise we saw how the glide path could be altered by changing the airspeed and the rotor r.p.m. In a spot autorotation the glide path can be altered by these methods and, in addition, the helicopter can be twisted and turned, cajoled and manoeuvred into the right position to reach the selected field by turning through 360° (given enough height), by downwind and crosswind flying followed by a turn in at the appropriate height, by "S" turns and by sideslipping.

Recovery to Powered Flight from Autorotative Flight

Provided the engine has not failed or been stopped, a recovery to powered flight is achieved as follows—

1. The rotor r.p.m. are checked. If they are above the maximum used in powered flight then they must be reduced to that figure by slightly raising the collective-pitch lever. If this is not done the engine will be over-speeded when the throttle is opened. When the lever is raised, the throttle must be used to prevent a sudden increase in engine r.p.m. due to cam action.

2. The throttle is opened carefully and the engine tachometer needle is brought up gently to meet the rotor tachometer needle.

3. The collective-pitch lever is raised to obtain the boost required. If the recovery is to a full power climb, which is excellent practice for students, there will be a considerable change of rudder pedal position necessary to maintain the heading and the stick will have to be used to control the longitudinal and lateral changes of trim.

Engine-off Landings

Following a descent in autorotation there are two ways of stopping the descent in order to make a safe landing, as follows—

1. By flaring, i.e. assuming the aircraft has forward speed, easing back on the stick and flattening the glide path. In this case fuselage energy is converted into rotor energy and lift. Whereas at high speed a flare could, if necessary, produce a momentary climb the only practical result of a flare at low speed would be to change the fuselage attitude. During a flare the r.p.m. tend to rise with the increase in g which is an advantage as the rotor is given more momentum for the final stage of the landing.

2. The collective-pitch lever can be raised. This means that inertia in the rotor is utilized to provide lift. Since the rotor decelerates rapidly when the lever is raised the lift gained is of short duration. In vertical descents there may be insufficient lift produced to stop the aircraft completely before it hits the ground.

In an engine-off landing either or both methods of stopping the descent could be used as follows—

FLARE ONLY. An aeroplane type of landing where, at high speed, the helicopter is flared gradually and flown on to the ground with the collective-pitch lever held down all the time. This is more of a theoretical than practical type of landing owing to the high ground speed on touching down, but it is perfectly feasible with some types of helicopter on good landing surfaces.

THE NO-FLARE TYPE. The fuselage is held level at a selected airspeed of 0 to 50 kt or so. As the aircraft nears the ground the collective-pitch lever is raised by an amount depending upon the rate of sink. Owing to the rapid descent, a fair amount of skill is required to make a good landing. If the lever is raised too early the rotor will lose r.p.m. rapidly with the aircraft several feet away from the ground and a heavy landing will result. An even heavier landing would result if the lever were raised too late. For a few seconds a certain flexibility is permitted in the use of the lever; for example, if the pilot does raise the lever too early he can lower it again and raise it a moment later. How long he can go on doing this depends upon the rate the rotor is losing r.p.m.

A combination of the two types of landing is generally preferred. The descent is carried out with forward airspeed. The glide path is flattened and the airspeed decreased by easing back on the stick. As the aircraft approaches the ground the fuselage is levelled fore and aft and the collective-pitch lever then raised to cushion the landing. Depending upon the technique used, the helicopter will touch down at zero ground speed or with a short run.

Engine-off landings following a failure of the engine at very low altitude, i.e. when hovering or air taxi-ing, can be accomplished safely owing to the inertia in the rotor, there being insufficient altitude to establish autorotation. The arrival is cushioned by the collective-pitch lever being raised. The tendency to turn due to the sudden change of torque at the time of the failure is corrected by use of the rudder pedals.

Limited Power Take-offs and Landings

When, owing to low air density, etc., a helicopter has insufficient power to take off in the normal manner it is often possible to utilize translational lift in order to become airborne and climb away. For practice purposes the exercise is carried out at a power slightly lower than that required to hover.

With the helicopter on the ground, power is increased to the maximum, or, in the case of a practice exercise, to the selected setting.

If the helicopter only just becomes airborne it may be possible to edge forward gradually, exchanging the ground cushion for translational lift, until a suitable airspeed is reached for climbing away. If not, and the helicopter has wheels or an undercarriage suitable for running along the ground, and the terrain is suitable, a running take-off is necessary. Holding the selected power the stick is eased forward and the helicopter accelerated along the ground. In this condition it may be running along the ground on the front wheel(s) only. When some airspeed has been gained and the aircraft feels light on the wheel(s) the stick is eased back and the helicopter flown level near the ground until sufficient airspeed has been gained for climbing away.

A limited power landing is carried out by maintaining forward airspeed down to a few feet above the ground, slowing down gradually and touching down as maximum power, or the selected power, is about to be reached. Generally the aircraft can be brought to a momentary hover under these circumstances, so, for practice, it is landed while there is still forward ground speed. After the touch-down ground resonance is a possibility to be guarded against.

High-altitude Flying

When flying at what, for a helicopter, would be termed high-altitude flying, certain differences are apparent in the handling qualities, as follows—

Climbing

1. During a continuous climb the r.p.m. and boost will tend to alter.

2. When full throttle height is reached maximum available power is maintained by keeping the throttle fully open, the r.p.m. then being controlled by the collective-pitch lever.

3. Above certain altitudes the best airspeed for climbing reduces progressively with altitude.

4. Above certain altitudes movements of the throttle will produce large rather unstable changes of boost.

5. With altitude the controls become less effective. This was particularly noticeable in earlier helicopters with rather insensitive controls and, on occasions, the stick could be alarmingly close to its stops.

Level Flight

1. The minimum airspeed to maintain level flight will increase with altitude, i.e. above a certain height it will not be possible to hover at maximum power, but height can be maintained with forward airspeed. The greater the height the greater becomes the minimum speed at which height can be maintained.

2. Owing to blade stall the maximum airspeed must be reduced progressively with height, and blade stall can occur with lower g forces in any manoeuvres.

3. Owing to the increasing ineffectiveness of the tail rotor with altitude more rudder must be held to balance the torque.

Autorotational Flight

1. The rotor r.p.m. will tend to be higher and must be retained within the limits by correct positioning of the collective-pitch lever. As altitude is lost, the lever should be progressively lowered to maintain the same r.p.m.

Quick Stops

The object of a quick stop is to come to the hover from cruising flight in the quickest possible time without gaining or losing height. It has a limited practical value, but it is excellent advanced co-ordination practice for students.

The quick stop is generally practised at about 30 ft above ground, or higher, and is commenced from level flight at cruising speed. To slow down, the stick is eased back. This tends to cause a climb, so collective-pitch must be reduced; the lever should be placed fully down unless the rotor r.p.m. approach their maximum limit. At this stage height is controlled by longitudinal positioning of the stick. If the result of lowering the lever is to cause a rise in engine r.p.m. these must be controlled by the throttle, but generally they are held at a convenient idling figure.

The helicopter should now be flying level in autorotation, the momentum of the fuselage providing a source of energy. As the aircraft slows down, the nose is progressively raised to prevent sink. When the point is reached where sinking cannot be prevented by this means powered flight must be reverted to in a similar manner to a recovery from normal autorotation. For a moment or two the aircraft is flying along with the tail well down and with considerable power output, the rotor acting as a highly efficient brake. As the aircraft comes to a halt the fuselage must be quickly placed in a normal hovering attitude and power reduced accordingly.

CHAPTER IX

HELICOPTER HISTORY

THE story of man's attempts to fly with rotary wings is a long one. The difficulties for the pioneers were such that the practical helicopter did not arrive until about thirty years after the first successful flight in powered aeroplanes. Indeed, the helicopter owes as much to the growth of aerodynamic knowledge gained from fixed wings as it does to overall improvements in mechanical engineering.

With the benefit of hindsight we can see that early ideas for rotary-wing flight were confused and full of misconceptions. Occasionally a touch of genius could be seen, but impractical concepts sometimes persisted for too long and good inventions were often discarded only to be retrieved later by others. Progress was frustrating, for as one major obstacle was overcome another would appear that would seem to be insurmountable.

It is reasonable to believe that the concept of fixed-wing flight predated that of rotary-wing flight. Ancient man watching the birds would obtain inspiration for flight by example; the notion of achieving a vertical and hovering capability by the use of horizontally rotating propellers must have come much later by a process of logic.

If projects, ideas, inventions and patents are taken in chronological sequence it may be seen how man's thoughts were directed and how contemporary knowledge and new discoveries influenced further development until helicopters became practical vehicles.

For the first known document concerning rotary-wing flight we must look to the fourth century AD for in the *Pao Phu Tau* we find the great Taoist and alchemist Ko Hung writing:

> Someone asked the Master about the principles (*tao*) of mounting to dangerous heights and travelling into the vast inane. The Master said, "Some have made flying cars (*fei chhe*) with wood from the inner part of the jujube tree, using ox-leather (straps) fastened to returning blades so as to set

the machine in motion (*huan chien i yin chhi chi*)."

Joseph Needham[1] (figures in square brackets refer to the Bibliography) writes:

> There can be no doubt that the first plan which Ko Hung proposes for flight is the helicopter top; "returning (or revolving) blades" can hardly mean anything else, especially in close association with a belt or strap. This kind of toy was termed in 18th century Europe the "Chinese top", though it seems to have been known in the West in late medieval times.

One can only marvel at the technology required to make this toy. Who made the first windmill? Was he inspired by watching sycamore leaves and the like? Who, knowing that the wind could turn a windmill, first reasoned that if a windmill were to be turned by a more palpable agency, then a wind could be produced? And who, in turn, realized that thrust and lift could now be created?

Projects and events of note from the fourth century AD to 1946 are as follows.

c. 320 AD   Ko Hung describes the Chinese flying top.

1490   Leonardo da Vinci, having spent some years trying to develop flying machines, designed a lifting screw made of starched linen (Fig. 112) and is therefore credited with being a pioneer helicopter designer.

1754   Lomonosov (Russia) is said to have proposed to the Russian Academy of Science a co-axial contra-rotating model operated by clockwork for lifting meteorological instruments.

1768   Paucton (France) revived da Vinci's ideas and designed a model he called a Ptérophore. It was to be man-powered and to have two aerial screws, one to sustain and one to propel.

1784   Fresh interest in vertical flight was aroused by Launoy and Bienvenu who demonstrated a model helicopter to the Académie des Sciences. The toy consisted of co-axial rotors powered by the spring loading of a whalebone bow (Fig. 113).

1796   Sir George Caley made his first model helicopter on the same lines as Launoy and Bienvenu. This also stimulated interest in flying, although there is no record of any helicopter designs of note for some years.

1818 Count Adolphe de Lambertgye suggested that a helicopter would communicate between his proposed ornith-opter-like airliner and the ground (Fig. 114).

1828 Vittorio Sarti (Italy) designed his Aereo Veliero. It was a co-axial type, the rotors being like large sails which were intended to be rotated by jets of steam coming from the rotor shaft.

1828 Mayer (Britain) attempted to build a man-powered helicopter.

1842 The development of the steam-engine gave new impetus to inventors and the first successful steam-driven model stands to the credit of an Englishman. "W. H. Phillips completed and flew successfully a helicopter model driven by steam jets from the rotor tips—like Hero's aeolipile—the jets being the result of the combustion of charcoal, nitre, and gypsum: it flew up fast and crossed two fields. Phillips showed a replica of this model at the 1868 Exhibition held by the Aeronautical Society at the Crystal Palace".[2]

1842 Robert Taylor wrote to Sir George Caley asking for his opinion of his design for a convertiplane. In essence this consisted of a model with co-axial rotors driven by steam power. The originality of his idea became apparent when altitude was gained, for then the wide-chord airscrews joined together to become an umbrella-like aerofoil, translational flight being achieved by the pull of a tractor airscrew.

1843 Sir George Caley made an improved helicopter top of the string-pull type. This flew to a height of 25 ft; a later improved model made by someone else is said to have reached 90 ft (Fig. 115). The same year he published a paper in which he presented his design for an "Aerial Carriage" (Fig. 116).

1843 Bourne (Britain) flew a model of Caley's Chinese top powered by watch springs.

1845 Cossus (France) designed a steam-powered helicopter with a main rotor and two small propellers for control and thrust (Fig. 117).

1846 Marc Seguin (France) experimented with a large lifting screw.

1847 Dr Van Hecke proposed a machine with four rotors.

1848 An anonymous writer in the U.S. publication *Scientific*

American described a multi-rotor helicopter design which had pusher propellers.

1859   Henry Bright designed a helicopter with co-axial rotors (Fig. 118).

1861   In an attempt to provide vertical control for balloons without the expenditure of either gas or ballast, Bright put forward the idea of suspending a "helicopter" beneath the car of the vehicle.

1861   Ponton d'Amécourt (France) designed a helicopter with sets of contra-rotating rotors and a propeller driven by steam. Vertical and horizontal planes were fitted at the rear for control purposes (Fig. 119).

1861   De la Landelle (France) proposed several designs for steam-driven large helicopters, one of which consisted of airscrews, inclined planes and parachutes.

1861   Mortimer Nelson (U.S.A.) proposed a helicopter which was to use a steam engine of 40 h.p. The aircraft had twin four-bladed rotors on outriggers and co-axial propellers in the nose for forward propulsion. In the event of mechanical failure a large circular frame with a cloth attached to it was intended to act as a parachute.

1861   Professor Mitchell (U.S.A.) attempted to develop a helicopter for use in the Civil War.

1862   W. C. Palmers (U.S.A.) constructed a model of a proposed helicopter which was to carry explosives.

1862   Ponton d'Amécourt built a more practical-looking steam-driven helicopter. This produced lift but did not become airborne (Fig. 120). He had more success with clockwork models, which flew well.

1863   Nadar (France) proposed a co-axial helicopter and produced a number of designs for steam-driven helicopters.

1870   Penaud (France) re-engined the helicopter top of Launoy and Bienvenu and of Sir George Caley by using elastic instead of a bow. Many flights were made.

1871   Pomés and De La Pauze suggested a helicopter driven by gunpowder, which had a rotor with adjustable pitch (Fig. 121).

1871   Blanchard (France) built a man-powered helicopter.

1871   Rykachev (Russia) conducted experiments with a four-bladed rotor.

1872   Renoir (France) experimented with a pedal-driven screw of 15 ft diameter.

1874   Achenbach (Germany) designed a steam-driven machine composed of a lifting airscrew, a propulsive airscrew, a rudder and a tail rotor (Fig. 122). This was the first time that a tail screw for anti-torque control had been mentioned in any design.

1874   The New York Novelty Works built a 2 h.p. co-axial rotor helicopter. The project was abandoned.

1877   Emmanuel Dieuaide experimented with a large co-axial model driven by steam. The boiler remained on the ground and the steam was taken to the aircraft by hosepipe (Fig. 123).

1877   Melikoff designed a helicopter driven by ether vapour, the rotor being shaped like a parachute. The idea was that the machine would screw itself upwards and parachute down. Translational thrust was provided by a propeller (Fig. 124).

1877   Enrico Forlanini (Italy) built a steam-driven model. It was the first shaft-driven, steam-powered helicopter model to leave the ground. The supply of power was unusual: the boiler, which consisted of a hollow sphere, was heated by external means and then attached to the helicopter and the throttle opened. Weight saving was achieved by this method and the model weighed only 7.7 lb. The aircraft had two co-axial rotors and the drive was connected to the top one only, the lower one being turned by torque reaction (Fig. 125).

1877   Delpred proposed a pedal-driven helicopter with a rotor for lift and a small propeller for thrust. Directional control was achieved by inclining the body, and therefore the c.g., in the direction intended.

1878   Emmanuel Dieuaide made a co-axial model driven by a small 2-cylinder steam engine. The rotors were permanently tilted for forward propulsion.

1878   P. Castel (France) built an elaborate compressed-air-driven model weighing 49 lb which had eight rotors arranged in two sets of four, contra-rotating. The compressed air was supplied from a ground reservoir through a flexible tube. The project was abandoned after crashing into a wall (Fig. 126).

1878   Dandrieux made and flew a series of little butterfly toys worked by rubber. The toys were lifted into the air by two or more rotors and would glide down on the butterfly wings. Dandrieux also designed a man-powered machine intended for vertical flight. It was something between a helicopter and an ornithopter. The wings moved on an oblique axis and the movements they made were something like a figure 8 (Fig. 127).

1880   Thomas Alva Edison (U.S.A.) began a number of experiments with models using electricity as the motive power. Results were disappointing but Edison always maintained that the helicopter would one day become a practical vehicle.

1885   R. G. Owen (Britain) proposed a side-by-side rotor configuration driven either manually or mechanically. Translational flight was to be achieved by tilting the body in the direction required.

1886   J. S. Foster (U.S.A.) produced a slightly more sophisticated design than that of Owen. It had reduction gearing and the drive shafts were to be tilted by manually-operated cords.

1889   J. Craig (Britain) proposed a turbine-driven tandem rotor system, powered by naphtha vapour.

1892   J. C. Walker proposed a system in which two rotors and two propellers were housed in vertical and horizontal cylinders respectively. Rudders at the end of the horizontal cylinders controlled yawing motion. Inclination of the machine for translational flight was carried out by an adjustable balance weight. A parachute was also provided.

1893   Sir Charles Parsons built a model with a single rotor and fixed vertical fins. The motive power was steam.

1895   E. C. de Los Olivos (Mexico) proposed a tandem rotor machine with a large adjustable wing surface for controlling translational flight.

1895   Sir Charles Parsons built a model of a steam-driven single-rotor helicopter.

1896   J. Roots proposed a single-rotor helicopter with torque-balancing rudder and a balance weight to tilt the machine in the required direction for translational flight. The rotor was built up from a tubular rim braced by wires and spokes to flanges on the vertical shaft. The blades, set at a pitch angle of approximately 20°, were formed of large pieces of fabric laced to the bracing wires.

1897 B. R. Beenan (Germany) patented a helicopter which had a single main rotor and a propeller for traction. The main interest in the machine is two-fold: like the Achenbach design of 1874 it had an anti-torque tail rotor; and it had collective-pitch control on both the main rotor and tail rotor. Provision was also made for tilting the rotor.

Despite the prescience of Achenbach and Beenan, most pioneers tried to overcome the problem of torque reaction by using two or more main rotors, a system that would also partially solve the problem of dissymmetry of lift in forward flight. Whilst limited success was achieved, in that some of the models actually became airborne, controlled translational flight was more difficult to attain. Until 1907 all helicopters which had flown had been models. Given the minimum knowledge of how a propeller worked and some form of power, be it steam, spring, clockwork, elastic, or inertia (as in the case of the string-pull type), it was not difficult to design a model lifting device. It was a much more complex exercise, however, to design and build a man-carrying helicopter capable of taking off, hovering and moving forward under control.

Until the latter quarter of the nineteenth century the intentions of designers had been frustrated by the lack of suitable engines. Power was there in the form of the steam engine, but the weight of the engine itself was prohibitive. It was not until N. A. Otto (Germany) invented the four-stroke internal combustion engine in 1876 that power-weight ratios became reasonable. Genius and perseverance brought about the first flight of a powered aeroplane in 1903, but before helicopter flight became a practical reality there were the mysteries of translational flight and stability to be solved.

1904 Renard (France) designed a helicopter with side-by-side rotors and driven by an internal combustion engine. He is credited with inventing the flapping hinge, but Cierva was unaware of this when he "reinvented" it (Fig. 128).

1904 Whitehead (U.S.A.) built a multi-rotor machine, but no flights were made.

1904 Leger, working in Monaco, built and flew a tethered electric helicopter for research into propellers. The rotor was driven by flexible shafting from electric motors on the ground.

1905 Emile Berliner (U.S.A.) attempted to build a helicopter having a co-axial system.

1906 Denny (Britain), Mumford and J. Pollock Brown built a six-rotor helicopter. The rotors were mounted side-by-side in pairs, each rotor of a pair intermeshing with the other. The rotor drive shafts could be tilted by cables (Fig. 129).

1906 Crocco (Italy) first suggested cyclic-pitch control.

1907 Otto Luyties (U.S.A.) tested a co-axial system.

1907 The Breguet-Richet No. 1 helicopter was built with four lifting rotors, each rotor consisting of four biplane blades. The machine became airborne, but had to be steadied by men holding it at all four corners (Fig. 130).

1907 Paul Cornu (France) made the world's first free flight in his helicopter. It was tandem-rotored with vanes in the downdraught for control. Despite Cornu's mark on history, the machine remained airborne for a maximum of seconds only and reached a height of about six feet (Fig. 131).

1908 The Breguet-Richet No. 2 flew to a height of 15 ft and flew forward for 60 ft. This machine had two rotors mounted on fixed wings. The rotors had a fixed forward tilt. The machine was completely unstable and crashed.

1908 Porter (Britain) designed a "helicopter". It was an unusual design, having a ducted fan system. Propellers blew air downwards through a large inverted cone.

1909 Fentum Phillips (Britain) experimented with a helicopter.

1909 Emile Berliner and J. Newton (U.S.A.) produced a helicopter powered by two engines each directly geared to two-bladed airscrews revolving in opposite directions. On three occasions the machine succeeded in lifting clear of the ground.

1910 Igor Sikorsky (Russia) built two unsuccessful helicopters (Fig. 132).

1910 Teasdale and Buckell (Britain) built a helicopter, a machine which was basically a monoplane with a rotor on each wing, the rotors being driven from the central engine. It is said to have become airborne.

1910   The Denny helicopter, now modified, carried out tethered hovering at 10 ft.

1911   Wyllie (Britain) built an unsuccessful helicopter.

1912   Boris Yuryev (Russia) built a small helicopter which had a single main rotor and a tail rotor. Work was abandoned after a main shaft broke during testing.

1912   Ellehammer (Denmark), who must rank as one of the geniuses amongst the world's aviation inventors, produced a co-axial helicopter with a tractor airscrew. It was one of the first to have cyclic-pitch control (Fig. 133).

1912   Papin and Rouilly (France) designed an amphibious helicopter. The rotor was to be driven by air jets from the blade tips. One variant had a single rotor blade which was balanced by the engine being installed on a stub blade as a counter-weight.

1914   The Denny helicopter, now on floats, flew 300 ft at a height of 10 ft and reached 15 knots. It was wrecked in a gale and was later abandoned as a result of the war.

1914–18   Von Karman and Petrosczy (Germany) with the Hungarian, Asboth, produced a lifting device intended to replace kite balloons for observation. It consisted of two superimposed lifting propellers. No control was provided and stability was achieved by mooring cables. It was initially powered by an electric motor, but was later powered by three 120 h.p. engines (Fig. 134).

1920   Pescara, an Argentinian working in Spain, built a co-axial machine which had biplane rotor blades. The lift was insufficient for the craft to become airborne.

1920   Oemichen (France) built a helicopter with two lifting airscrews to which a balloon was later added.

1921   Du Bothezat, another former Russian, carried out trials for the U.S. Army. His four-rotor machine had the axes of the rotors inclined inwards slightly in order to obtain horizontal stability in a similar manner to the dihedral of an aeroplane. The original design had two propellers for propulsion, and also had a centrally-mounted propeller rotating horizontally which gave some lift and was also intended to provide a braking effect to prevent the four rotors overspeeding during a descent. These features were removed in a later version. The machine carried out more than a hundred flights which, as it had only a 180 h.p. (later 220 h.p.) engine to lift its 3,600 lb, was quite an achievement (Fig. 135).

1922   Oemichen, using lessons learned from his first helicopter, built his second. Fig. 136 shows the rather complex design with four rotors and many propellers.

1923   Henry Berliner (U.S.A.), following in his father's foot-steps, built a side-by-side system with a propeller on a vertical axis for elevator control. Movable flaps in the down-wash were used for lateral control. The machine did become airborne but lacked stability and control.

1923   Perry (U.S.A.) built a helicopter which had a co-axial system. It was not a success.

1924   The Oemichen No. 2 established a distance record of 525 metres.

1924   Pescara, now working in France, established a distance record of 736 metres with his No. 3 machine (Fig. 137). His machine was remarkable in that both cyclic-pitch and collective-pitch were used. Pescara was one of the first to understand autorotation and his aircraft should have been able to descend safely in the event of engine failure.

1924   The Oemichen machine remained airborne for 14 minutes and also completed the first 1 kilometre closed circuit by a helicopter in 7 minutes 40 seconds.

1924   Von Baumhauer (Holland) built a single-rotor heli-copter with a tail rotor. Unfortunately he provided a second engine to drive the tail rotor instead of gearing it to the main engine. The weight penalty was such that the machine never rose more than a few feet.

1924   Brennan (Britain) built an experimental helicopter. It was one of the first to have a torqueless drive, for the rotor was driven by small propellers on the tips of two of the four blades. Compressed air was used to power the control system. Cyclic-pitch control was provided by blade warping caused by small aerodynamic tabs on the blades. It made many short flights before crashing in 1925 (Fig. 138).

1926   Isacco (Italy) tried to build a helicopter with torqueless rotors using the same principle as Brennan. He called his machine a "Helicogyre".

1926   Zaschka (Germany) designed a helicopter which incorporated a gyroscope to aid stability and to store up energy for engine-off landings. A swivelling propeller at the rear provided propulsion and rudder control.

It will be seen that although there were several projects which showed promise in the early 1920s, even the most successful helicopters could do little more than drift forward at slow speed. The world still awaited a practical helicopter.

A fact not always appreciated was that if a helicopter was produced that could become airborne, the flying would be carried out by pilots who had had no experience of helicopter piloting. Some of the instability reported or shown on film might have been controllable if the pilot had had some previous helicopter experience.

We must now turn our attention away from helicopters for a while and meet someone who, although he never built them, influenced their progress more than any other man. The substantial impact which he made on aviation endures long after his untimely death. Juan de la Cierva, alone among those rotary-wing pioneers struggling to find a way through the jungle of doubt and confusion, took a fresh path in a new direction and led others through to the broad road that lay ahead. Of him, Wing Commander Brie once said: "It appears fitting, when we meet to discuss one or the other of many aspects of rotary wing flight, that we should direct our thoughts to the one man (alas no longer with us) whose creative ability and genius not only made possible the Autogiro; but whose foresight and tenacity of purpose so well and truly laid the foundations upon which the helicopter now so surely stands."[6]

Cierva was born in Murcia, Spain, in 1895. His father was Minister of War for a spell and Cierva himself was a member of parliament in Spain on two occasions. His father was a rich man and provided initial financial backing for Juan's projects, the first of which was a glider. Juan and his brother had some narrow escapes due to lack of flying speed. Cierva said that the problem of removing the stall from aviation seemed to pursue him throughout his experimental work.

In 1912 Cierva built a power-driven biplane, and in 1913 a monoplane. A more ambitious effort in 1918 was a large three-engined biplane which was wrecked following a stall. In 1919 he hit on the idea of using windmills, or rotors, instead of wings and started to build a whole series of gyroplanes, or Autogiros, as he eventually called his products.

The Cierva number one, or C.1. (Fig. 139) had two contra-rotating co-axial rotors. The controls consisted of an elevator, a rudder, and a single aileron mounted vertically on top of the axis of the two rotors.

It must be remembered that in Cierva's machines the rotors were not power driven, the power going to a normal tractor propeller in the nose of the aircraft. Except for an initial starting rotation the rotors were driven by the airflow only, so they were autorotating. Hence one of the major problems which beset early helicopter designers, that of torque reaction, did not affect Cierva's aircraft. However, he was deeply concerned with the second major problem of rotary-wing aircraft—that of dissymmetry of lift. This is the rolling couple which occurs when a rotary wing aircraft moves forward: the advancing blade, the one moving into the direction of flight, has more airspeed than the retreating blade and so gains more lift (see Chapter VI).

Cierva found that the lower rotor of his C.1 ran at two-thirds the speed of the upper one, so his scheme to balance the rolling couple by using two rotors in this configuration would not work. He thought of connecting the two rotors by a differential gear, but came to the conclusion that a solution with a single rotor was better.

The C.2 (Fig. 140), with very wide chord blades, had a form of cyclic-pitch control to overcome the rolling couple, but the blades were not of sufficient torsional rigidity to react to the constant alternate twisting motion at the roots. The machine was reconstructed nine times, so it is little wonder that Cierva almost despaired of ever finding a solution to his problem.

The next step was in 1922 with the C.3 (Fig. 141), in which he attempted to brace the blades by means of high-tensile steel wires and to overcome the rolling problem by fitting a large elevator. This was divided into two different parts, right and left, so that they acted rather like ailerons as well as an elevator. Although the aircraft was rebuilt four times, the "elevator" was never able to overcome the problem.

The same year he hit on the idea which was perhaps his greatest contribution to rotary-wing flight—flapping hinges. Each rotor blade was hinged in a horizontal plane at its root and was therefore free to flap up and down. As explained more fully in Chapter VI, the advancing blade would, with increased airflow, lift itself up about the flapping hinge, thereby decreasing its angle of attack, while the retreating blade would flap down, thereby increasing its angle of attack; thus the net lifting effect on each blade root would be the same.

Flapping hinges were used for the blades of the C.4 (Fig. 142) and lateral control was intended to be provided by the pilot manually tilting the rotor axis, but the pilot's strength proved insufficient. The aircraft was reconstructed or modified fifteen times and lateral control was eventually provided by ailerons mounted on thin streamlined spars.

In January 1923 Cierva's Autogiro flew across Getafe airfield at a height of several metres, and later at nearby Cuatro Vientos airfield Lt. Gomez Spencer carried out an officially observed flight.

The next machine, the C.5, was satisfactory but was wrecked in a taxi-ing accident.

The Spanish government now became interested and advanced money to enable Cierva to build his C.6 (Fig. 143) single-seater research aircraft. This was based on an Avro 504 fuselage (110 h.p. Le Rhone engine) with a wider than standard undercarriage. The four-bladed rotor, with blades which were free to flap, was mounted on a pylon of steel tubes.

At the invitation of H. E. Wimperis, Director of Scientific Research at the Air Ministry, Cierva brought his third C.6 to Britain where Captain Courtney convincingly demonstrated it to a distinguished Farnborough gathering on 15 October 1925.

In 1926 Cierva formed his own company in Britain, the Cierva Autogiro Company, much of the finance for which was provided by Lord Weir and his brother, Air Commodore J. G. Weir. Thereafter the Cierva Autogiro Co. concentrated on the rotor system while the majority of the fuselage construction was carried out by A. V. Roe. In the ensuing years licences were granted to manufacturers in Britain, France, Germany, Japan and the U.S.A. to build Autogiros of the Cierva type. Many variations and improvements took place. In 1927 the C.8R (Fig. 144) was fitted with drag hinges, as it was found that flapping blades caused an oscillation in azimuth at the blade roots which could cause stress and subsequent blade fatigue failure. The fitting of drag hinges brought about another host of problems due to ground resonance, and drag dampers of the friction type were fitted.

During his development of the Autogiro, Cierva tried various methods of starting the rotor prior to the take-off run. In the early days the Autogiro used to be taxied round the airfield to obtain an airflow through the rotor and an initial rotation. The next development was to use a rope and drum method for initial rotation and about 50 per cent of the necessary r.p.m. was obtained in this way. A biplane blade fitted to the tail and inclined upwards to deflect the slipstream from the tractor propeller was then used, and with this device 60–70 per cent of the flying r.p.m. was gained. In the C.19 (Figs. 145 and 146) a final solution was at last achieved: a direct drive to the rotor from the engine was installed so that the rotor could be initially accelerated and then declutched at the commencement of the take-off run.

In 1927 Cierva took flying lessons at Hamble and thereafter assisted in the development flying of his own aircraft; he was in fact the pilot of the first rotary-wing aircraft to cross the Channel in 1928.

In 1933 the C.30 Autogiro (Fig. 147), later to be given the service name of Rota 1 by the R.A.F., was produced with direct control of the rotor by means of a column suspended from the head of the rotor pylon which acted directly on the blades through a tilting-hub control. This was, in fact, a form of cyclic-pitch control. The pilot did not forcibly tilt the rotor, but applied cyclic-pitch changes to the blades, causing them to lift themselves up and down during their rotation, effectively tilting the rotor disc. Prior to this, all Cierva's successful Autogiros had been controlled in roll and pitch by conventional ailerons mounted on wings or supports and an elevator at the tail; a system which worked well at normal airspeeds but which had marked limitations at speeds under about 20 knots.

The same year a C.30 was converted for jump-start trials. The production model of the jump take-off Autogiro was the C.40 (Fig. 148), named the Rota II by the R.A.F. In this type, in order to take-off, the blades were accelerated in fine pitch by the engine which was declutched when the optimum r.p.m. were attained. With the loss of torque the blades would swing forward on angled drag hinges and automatically increase their pitch, the consequent sudden increase in lift from the rotor causing the aircraft to leap into the air. The pilot would then immediately gain forward airspeed in order to continue the autorotation of the rotor. In this manner the Autogiro would, for a few moments, become a helicopter relying on the rotor inertia alone in order to become airborne.

The performance of Cierva's Autogiros improved as the years went by. The 68 m.p.h. of the C.6 was increased until 110 m.p.h. was reached in the C.30. In marked contrast to similar developments in fixed-wing aircraft, the landing speed remained the same throughout the period.

In 1936 Cierva was killed when taking off in fog at Croydon as a passenger in an airliner. His loss was a sad blow to all who knew him. A gifted linguist, he was a brilliant man whose infectious enthusiasm inspired all who knew him. The magazine *Flight* of the period stated: "One of his great charms was his modesty. He never promised more than he could fulfil and he was that *very* unusual type of inventor: the man who knew more about the theory and practice than anyone else. He had the courage of his convictions and learned to fly his own machines, not merely tolerably, but extremely well. No better way of honouring his memory could be imagined than to carry to its ultimate solution the great work which he started."

One has but to look at any helicopter today to see his memorial.

Let us now revert to the chronological sequence to see how others progressed during and after Cierva's time.

1928   Asboth built his fourth helicopter which had two wooden screws mounted co-axially. Control was provided by six surfaces hanging in the downdraught and moving about horizontal hinges. It was a crude machine, owing nothing to Cierva, but it did climb to 100 ft and flew 3,000 yds at a speed of 12 m.p.h. (Fig. 151).

1928   Pitcairn made the first Autogiro flight in America.

1930   D'Ascanio (Italy) built one of the most successful heilcopters of the period. It was a co-axial machine with flapping hinges. Cyclic-pitch control was achieved by means of tabs on the trailing edges of the blades, warping them as required. Three small auxiliary airscrews provided yawing, lateral and longitudinal control. Records were set up for altitude, duration and distance, being 60 ft, 8 minutes 45 seconds, and 560 yds respectively.

1930   Hafner (Austria) flew his R.1 single-rotor helicopter, which he built in collaboration with Nagler. The torque was balanced by two large vanes aft of the cockpit and in the rotor downdraught. Collective-pitch and cyclic-pitch changes were achieved through a swash plate. Only short flights were achieved as it was difficult to master the large gyroscopic moments of the rotor.

1930   Bleeker (U.S.A.) built a single-rotor helicopter with four blades and a propeller on each blade in the style of Brennan and Isacco.

1932   The Kay gyroplane flew (Fig. 149). It had collective-pitch control, normal elevators for longitudinal control and cyclic-pitch for lateral control.

1932   In Russia, research into rotary-wing aircraft had been taking place at the TsAGI under Yuriev, Bratukhin featuring prominently in the development. A helicopter with a single main rotor and two small rotors at nose and tail was flown. It crashed in 1933.

1932   Hafner moved to Britain with his R.II helicopter where flapping hinges were fitted to the blades. This improved control in roll and pitch (Fig. 152).

1932   Flettner's (Germany) helicopter No. 1 made a successful tethered take-off. Its two-bladed rotor had propellers on each blade in a similar manner to the helicopters of Brennan, Isacco and Bleeker.

1933   Florine's (Belgium) helicopter flew. It had tandem rotors both turning in the same sense. Torque was balanced by tilting the rotors to one side.

1933   The Weir W.1. (Britain) gyroplane flew. C. and J. Weir Ltd built Autogiros under licence from the Cierva Autogiro Co. The W.1 had direct control, flapping and drag hinges on the blades, and mechanical drive for starting the rotor. The W.2 was basically similar with a bigger engine.

1933   The Breguet-Dorand (France) helicopter first flew (Fig. 153). It will be remembered that Breguet first attempted to build a helicopter in 1907. In between his helicopter efforts he became famous as a designer of aeroplanes. He now produced a co-axial machine which had both cyclic-pitch and collective-pitch control. Directional control was by differential collective pitch.

1935   The Breguet-Dorand helicopter bettered all the D'Ascanio records and also set up a straight course speed record of 27 m.p.h.

1935   Hafner's (Britain) A.R.III Gyroplane flew (Fig. 150). The blades had flapping hinges and cyclic- and collective-pitch control were provided by spider arms. This gyroplane was a jump-start type and was unusual in that the collective pitch was under the full control of the pilot. Not only could the amount of the jump be controlled but landings could be more gentle and the aircraft could be kept firmly on the ground by decreasing the pitch after touch-down. Blade suspension was achieved by means of torsionally flexible tie rods. This success-ful feature was used by Hafner on his subsequent Bristol helicopters.

1935   Flettner's F1 184 gyroplane flew.

1936   Weir's W.3 gyroplane flew. This was a two-bladed jump-start model and used the angled drag hinge (Fig. 155) for the jump in a similar manner to that of the C.40. The W.4 was an improved version of the W.3.

1936   Flettner's F1 185 helicopter flew. This had a single main rotor with two small anti-torque propellers on outriggers on each side of the cabin.

1936   The Breguet-Dorand helicopter reached a speed of 62 m.p.h.

1936   The Focke-Wulf Fw 61 flew (Fig. 154). The Germans now came to the forefront of rotary-wing flight with a convin-cing demonstration of a practical helicopter. Doctor Focke had gained rotary-wing experience when Germany built C.19 and C.30 Autogiros under licence. He started building scale models of helicopters and then created the Fw 61. This machine had side-by-side fully articulated rotors on outriggers. Cyclic pitch was used for longitudinal control, differential pitch for directional control and differential collective pitch for lateral control. Vertical control was achieved by varying the rotor r.p.m. with the throttle—a method that is generally too sluggish to be entirely satisfactory.

1937   The Fw 61 made its first autorotative landing.

1937   The Breguet-Dorand made its first autorotative landing.

1937   The Fw 61 established several world records including a speed of 76 m.p.h. over a closed circuit. The same year it gave a much publicised demonstration inside the Berlin Sports Stadium.

1937   The Nagler (Austria) Helicogyro was tested in Britain. The rotor could be driven by the engine, torque reaction being balanced by the slipstream from a pusher propeller acting on a rudder. When airborne the machine could be flown as an autogyro.

1937   The Herrick Convertiplane (U.S.A.) was flown as a gyroplane. Conversion to an aeroplane configuration was never carried out.

1938   The Weir W.5 helicopter (Britain) flew. The chief designer was C. G. Pullin. This was the first successful British helicopter and had a similar lay-out to the Fw 61. It was extremely small, having an all-up weight of only 860 lb. 80 hours of flying were carried out and a speed of 70 m.p.h. was reached (Fig. 156).

1939   The Weir W.6 flew. This was a scaled-up version of the W.5 and was the first two-seat helicopter in the world. The war curtailed its development (Fig. 157).

1939   The Flettner F1 265 flew. It had side-by-side inter-meshing rotors.

1939   Igor Sikorsky flew his VS 300 (Fig. 158).

It will be remembered that Sikorsky had previously built unsuccessful helicopters in Russia before the First World War. In the interim period he had built his well-known flying boats and had emigrated to America. The VS 300 was unique because not only was it the first aircraft of this configuration (main rotor with tail rotor) to fly successfully, but its production version, the R.4, marked the commencement of the helicopter industry in the U.S.A.

The story of the VS 300 development should be told in Sikorsky's own words:

It was of very simple construction, being built of welded steel, but was capable of easy adjustment, thereby enabling valuable information to be obtained. This aircraft had a very interesting life of about four years, during which time it was tested extensively. I was the test pilot during the first flight in October, 1939. It had a single main rotor with an anti-torque rotor at the tail. This aircraft was crashed about two months after the first flight as a result of which the cyclic pitch control, which was installed in the first helicopter, was discarded and we went for control by way of auxiliary rotors. We fixed two additional lifting rotors at the rear end, where also was mounted a third rotor for balancing torque and directional control. The operation of both of these lifting rotors in the same direction gave longitudinal control, in the opposite direction gave lateral control. After various experiments, by the end of 1940 the machine was able to stay up 15 minutes or so. About that time a minor trouble was the subject of a discussion I had with the President of United Aircraft. He had mentioned that the aircraft was flying well sideways and backwards, but he had not seen the machine flying forwards like other aircraft, to which I replied: "Sir, that is a minor engineering problem that we have not yet succeeded in solving."

Later on we arranged to fly forward very well because we found that when controlling by means of auxiliary rotors, the auxiliary rotor should not be placed in the slipstream above the main rotor. After early trials with auxiliary rotors in front, they were placed at the tail and were all right. Rearwards flying of the machine was very successful. However, we decided, in making the next ship, to replace the two rotors by a combination which presented a more or less tandem rotor helicopter with one large and one small rotor besides a small tail rotor. This craft gave very satisfactory results and could gradually be accelerated to a higher speed, which was of the order of 75 m.p.h.

Early in 1942 we had a two-seater helicopter for the Army ready, with full cyclic-pitch control. This machine, the R.4, is well known and has given very satisfactory results.

1940   The Focke Achelis Fa 223 (Drache) flew. This was a development of the Fw 61 and reached a record height of 23,294 ft. Most of the production models were destroyed in Allied air attacks.

1940   Nagler and Rolz (Austria) built a helicopter with a single-bladed rotor. The engine was mounted on an arm to balance the weight of the single blade, and the blade itself was driven by two airscrews mounted upon it.

1941   The Platt-Le Page (U.S.A.) flew. It was similar to the Fw 61.

1941   Nagler and Rolz (Austria) built a very small helicopter having a two-bladed rotor and with an engine on each blade.

1941   The Flettner 282 (Kolibri) flew (Fig. 159). Like its predecessors, it had side-by-side intermeshing rotors. Interesting features were the automatic control of rotor r.p.m. by blade pitch changes and the automatic change to autorotative pitch in the event of engine failure. Altogether Anton Flettner could claim considerable success with his helicopters. The Fl 282 was used operationally from 1942.

1941   The Rotachute (Britain) was developed by Hafner. This was a small rotary-wing glider intended to replace the parachute in certain roles. Carried in an aircraft in a folded state, it opened automatically after ejection and could then make a controlled descent. Although about twenty were produced, this aircraft never became operational (Fig. 160).

1942   The Sikorsky R.4 first flew (Plate V). This was the successful production version of the VS 300 and the first helicopter to be produced in any numbers. It had side-by-side seating for two pilots, and not only did many pilots receive training in it but it demonstrated the potential of the helicopter to the world.

1942   The Fa 330 (Germany) was a collapsible autogyro kite designed by Dr Klages for use from submarines for observation purposes. It was stored in a watertight cylinder on deck when not in use. It was superior to balloons in that it could not be seen so easily and could be stowed more readily (Fig. 162).

1943   The Doblhoff 342 VI and V2 flew (Fig. 163). These were built to the design of Doblhoff, Stepan and Laufer and were the first helicopters to use tip-jet drive on the rotor blades successfully.

1943   The Omega 2MG (Russia) flew. It was similar to the Fw 61, but had twin engines.

1943   The first Bell (U.S.A.) helicopter flew. This was the first of thousands of Bell helicopters of all shapes and sizes that have since been built. The famous stabilizer bar was the brainchild of Arthur Young who first worked on electrically powered model helicopters in the 1930s. He gained support for building full-sized aircraft after demonstrating one of his models to Lawrence Bell in 1941.

1943   The Rotabuggy or Flying Jeep (Britain) flew. A development of the Rotachute, it consisted of a truck fitted with a rotor and a stabilizing fin. The intention was for these machines to be towed behind aircraft and then released over the required territory. Considerable problems were encountered with control, stability and vibration (Fig. 161).

1943   Piasecki PV2 flew. This was the first of Piasecki's many helicopters and was the only one he built with a single main rotor. (His subsequent helicopters were of tandem rotor configuration.)

1944   The first Sikorsky R.4s arrived in Britain for the Royal Navy.

1944   The Cierva W.9 (Britain) flew. Designed by C. G. Pullin, this experimental machine had an anti-torque jet at the tail. This jet could, by the use of deflectors, also affect the trim of the aircraft about the lateral and longitudinal axes. The main rotor was mounted on a constant-velocity joint and had tilting hub control.

1944   The Kellett (U.S.A.) XR5 flew. This had side-by-side intermeshing rotors.

1945   The Doblhoff WNF 342 V4 flew. Experience with the first two Doblhoff models had shown that fuel consumption was extremely high. The V4 was intended to remedy this by using the tip-drive for take-off only, the aircraft changing to the gyroplane condition in forward flight with the forward thrust being provided by a pusher airscrew (Fig. 164).

1945   First helicopter crossing of the English channel, carried out by an Fa 223.

HELICOPTER PROGRESS SINCE 1946

Since the war, development followed a predictable route, although a frustratingly slow one for those people already convinced of the helicopter's potential. Designers set out to improve the machines in every aspect. Occasionally they explored paths which led nowhere; or they were hindered by lack of funds or unexpected technical obstacles like intolerable noise. It was the Korean war which really proved to the doubters that the helicopter was indispensable, and the vehicle is now an essential tool for the armed forces and many civil operators. Indeed, there are more helicopters than fixed-wing aircraft in the world's air forces.

A selection of improvements and other features are discussed briefly below under various headings.

Configurations

By 1946 it had been realized that almost any reasonable helicopter configuration was capable of flight, and many were tried. The Cierva Air Horse was an example of a three-rotored type, but vibration troubles, economic considerations, complexity of the systems and a fatal crash caused abandonment of the project. From time to time a designer here or there revives the co-axial contra-rotating system, but this type seldom goes into large-scale production in the western world. The Fairey Aviation Company produced its Gyrodyne, an ambitious project by Dr Bennett, in which the conventional anti-torque rotor was replaced by a tractor airscrew fitted at the tip of a stub wing. When accelerating forward, power to the main rotor could be progressively reduced until the airscrew became the sole means of propulsion. The aircraft was then operating as an autogyro. This produced the hoped-for speed benefit and in 1948 the Gyrodyne gained the world helicopter speed record. Fairey's next project was the compound helicopter, the Rotodyne, which combined a tip-jet-driven rotor for slow speed and hovering flight and the gyroplane principle for fast forward flight, two airscrews providing not only the forward thrust but also the yaw control at slow speed. Economic considerations forced the end of this complicated vehicle.

Some conventional helicopters employed torqueless rotors using tip-jet drive, with vanes in the down-wash for rudder control, but it was generally found that a small tail rotor was more satisfactory.

By far the most plentiful type manufactured has been the single main rotor with a torque-balancing tail rotor, first used successfully in production by Sikorsky; the tandem-rotored type is numerically second.

A recent return to the side-by-side rotor system has been made, in particular, by Russia, whose Mi 12, a four-engined giant, has lifted a payload of nearly forty tons. In common with some recent helicopters it has fixed wings for partially un-loading the rotors in forward flight.

Convertiplane projects are increasing in number: the *tilt-wing* machine resembles a fixed-wing aircraft and has propellers or rotors on the leading edges of the wings. For take-off and hovering flight the wings and the rotor drive shafts are in the vertical position. By gradually tilting the wings forward, translational flight is gained; when sufficient speed is reached the wings are providing all the lift and the rotors, now acting as propellers, are providing all the thrust. In the *tilt-rotor* machine the rotors are mounted at the tips of relatively small wings. The wings remain fixed at all times. On attaining a basic forward speed the rotors can be tilted forward until they are acting as propellers. In the event of total engine failure the aircraft should be able to revert to the helicopter configuration and make an autorotative landing.

Among recent unusual designs there is found the drone type of small remotely piloted helicopters (R.P.H.) which can be used as aerial platforms (like the Karman Petrosczy of World War I). These may be either tethered types which are controlled by electrical signals or radio, or free and radio controlled. Their main use is for reconnaissance and communication purposes. In naval vessels they can increase the strike range of missiles by elevating the radar control above normal mast height. When one learns that an American R.P.H. has attained a tethered height of 10,000 ft, the potential appears consider-able. A Fokker design has turbo compressors providing compressed air to the blade tips of a co-axial system. The Marchetti Heliscope is powered by electricity through a cable from the ground, and the Marchetti Rotormobile uses tip-jet drive. The Dornier Kiebitz tethered platform operates from a lorry or tank and the Dornier Seekiebitz from ships. Remote control has also been used for conventional helicopters and autogyros with commands transmitted either by wire or radio.

The gyroplane has staged an impressive comeback and many firms are producing them. A jump take-off facility has been provided in several. The Kaman Saver is a gyroplane with telescopic blades. This remarkable machine is intended to allow a military pilot to eject from his fixed-wing aircraft and, using the Saver, to fly 50 nautical miles at 100 knots towards friendly territory.

The Aerocrane project is a hybrid vehicle that combines the

lift capability of a helium-filled balloon with the lift and control of a helicopter. It consists of a balloon with rotor blades projecting from it, and these blades have both cyclic- and collective-pitch capability. When power is applied, the entire balloon-rotor combination rotates, thereby increasing the lift and making control possible.

Size

In 1945, the S.51, which lifted a pilot and three passengers, was considered a large helicopter. By today's standards it is a fairly small one. There are, of course, even smaller ones, some of which carry only one man. In contrast, the world's largest is the Mil Mi 12 with a fuselage length of 37 metres and a height of 12.5 metres. The world record for weight lifting is equal to the weight of five hundred men.

Engines

The normal internal combustion piston engine is still in use to a fair extent in small helicopters, but the gas turbine is being increasingly used in the majority of new aircraft. There are about two dozen ways in which the gas turbine is superior to the piston engine, but only a few disadvantages such as the initial cost and the fact that the ingestion of foreign matter, which can happen during hovering manoeuvres, may cause extensive damage. The fitting of the recently developed vortex tube sand filter, however, has gone a long way towards overcoming this latter problem.

Many designers have tried tip-jet drive, using rockets, ram jets, pulse jets and ducted pulse jets. In these cases the engines are located on the blade tips. Other possibilities are the use of pressure jet systems and gas-stream generators, in which cases part of the jet equipment is in the fuselage and ducted blades are necessary. Tip-mounted turbojets have not yet been used, the high centrifugal loads and large gyroscopic moments being a major problem. Projects having tip-jet drive are continually cropping up, but never stay for long; the complexities of transmitting fuel or gas through a rotating joint and along the rotor blades are considerable—although the problem was solved in the Rotodyne. The high fuel consumption is another drawback.

The technique of flight refuelling from other aircraft has been perfected. Helicopters can also be refuelled while airborne from moving ships, or from floating bags of fuel left by surface craft in strategic positions.

The single-engined helicopter of the 1940s has, naturally, been followed by twin- and multi-engined types. Even some small helicopters have been given twin engines.

Rotor Blades

In tne early 1940s, rotor blades generally consisted of a main spar with metal or wooden ribs with a fabric cover; or they were of laminated wood. To obtain a matching set of blades was not easy. Following this, the trend was for blades to be all metal. They comprised a spar, which might also be the leading edge, and a wrap-round outer skin; alternatively the spar might have pockets, forming the trailing edge, bonded to it. Composite materials such as glass– or carbon–fibre have also been used. Tail-rotor blades, which used to be of laminated wood, later tended to be of metal or of fibreglass; carbon fibre and laminated glass resin also being used in some parts.

There is now a strong tendency for the use of plastics in rotor blades, especially in the small-to-medium range of helicopter. This makes the blades simpler and more economic to produce especially when complicated aerofoil sections are required. It is claimed that plastic blades have an unlimited life.

Emphasis on minimizing the effects of battle damage has resulted in the production of blades of multi-spar construction so that damage to one spar will not result in catastrophic failure. In the Bell Advanced Attack Helicopter the multi-spar system is employed in blades of unusually low aspect ratio.

Whereas rotor blades used to be fairly flexible in vertical bending movements along the span, many of them now tend to be much stiffer. Glass fibre blades, however, are more flexible than metal blades and they rely on high centrifugal forces to give them rigidity when rotating.

Some aircraft have systems for detecting incipient blade failure in their metal or glass-fibre blades. One such system is the blade inspection method (B.I.M.). The blade spars are airtight and filled with nitrogen under pressure. A loss of pressure caused by a crack or hole operates an indicator which can be found on inspection. Another similar system is the integrated spar inspection system (I.S.I.S.), which utilizes a vacuum instead of nitrogen under pressure. A loss of vacuum produces a visual indication.

The problem of icing on rotor blades and on other parts of the helicopter has been the subject of intensive research and testing. To a certain extent, rotor blades have their own partial de-icing system due to vibration, flexing and centrifugal force; but ice accretion can still be dangerous. A major problem has been the ingestion by the engine of pieces of ice from the airframe. Thermal, chemical and mechanical means have been used for protection of the blades and other parts. Ice accretion has been reduced in the rotor hub by cleaner design. Baffles have been used to prevent impingement on vital moving parts and engine intakes.

In some high performance aircraft, experiments have been made with rotor blades that have swept-back tips. This feature enables the advancing blade tip to approach the speed of sound more closely.

Rotor Systems

The trend is for neater rotor heads, especially in small- and medium-sized helicopters. The profusion of push-pull rods, bearings, swash plates, etc., for changing pitch have often been replaced by one or two actuating arms, the mechanism for operating them being hidden from view. Considerable developments have been made in rotor systems in which the blades have no individual flapping and drag hinges, their functions being carried out by flexible blade elements either located in the blade root or forming part of the hub. In some designs the high centrifugal loads, which used to be borne by pitch-change bearings, are now carried by torsionally flexible tie bars. Where these are used, the pitch-change bearings may remain, but as they bear only radial loads they are journal bearings and not thrust bearings. A recent method of simplifying the conventional-hinged rotor system is the replacement of hinges by elastomeric (metal and rubber laminate) bearings.

Experiments have been carried out by Sikorsky with the A.B.C. (Advancing Blade Concept) rotor. Two rotors are necessary for this and Sikorsky uses a co-axial system. The rotor blades are made as rigid as possible so that flapping is minimal. There is no compensation for dissymmetry of lift in forward flight in the individual rotors; instead, the rolling couples from the two rotors cancel each other. This means that the advancing blades can be allowed to generate considerable lift while the retreating blades have little or none. The main advantage of the system is that more thrust is generated and higher aircraft speeds should be possible.

Experiments have been carried out with the Reversing Velocity Rotor (R.V.R.). One of the factors preventing high helicopter speeds is the reverse airflow over the retreating blades (coupled with the stall developing at the blade tips) as speed is increased. The R.V.R. is a system where at high forward speeds an additional cyclic-pitch capability is given to the retreating blade so that it has a negative pitch angle. With respect to the airflow, however, it has a positive angle of attack. In this type of rotor the blades must have aerofoil sections suitable for airflow in either direction.

Another idea which is the subject of research is the Circulation Control Rotor (C.C.R.). This employs air blown through thin slots on both the leading and trailing edges of the rotor blades for both "collective" and "cyclic" control. There are many possible versions of this theme ranging from blades supporting the system, to spars with few aerodynamic properties which merely carry the air pipes and vents.

Modern rotors generally have more useful inertia due to higher tip speeds. This enables engine-off landings to be carried out more easily.

Among recent developments, the Aérospatiale Starflex Rotor must be mentioned. All main load-bearing parts are made of glass reinforced plastics. With elastomeric bearings the rotor head requires no lubrication, it has few components, is inexpensive and is simple to maintain.

Variable diameter rotors are the subject of research.

Large helicopters, especially naval versions, often have cockpit-controlled, powered, blade-folding devices. Other smaller ship-borne helicopters may have manual blade folding. (A manual folding capability is generally provided for the tail in all naval helicopters.)

For some years, many rotor systems that use flapping hinges on the blades have had retractable droop stops and retractable flapping restrainers. These function when the aircraft is on the ground and the blades are turning slowly or have stopped. The flapping restrainers prevent the blades rising in an uncontrollable manner in high or gusty wind conditions. When the rotor starts to turn and the r.p.m. rise above a certain figure the restrainers are withdrawn by the action of centrifugal force acting on small weights. The retractable droop stops replace the old fixed stops. Their normal duty is to hold the blades in an approximately horizontal position while the rotor is turning slowly or is static. When the rotor r.p.m. rise above a pre-determined figure, the stops retract and the blades are free to flap as required.

The tail rotor has been subject to several developments. A few projects have systems which enable the thrust to be altered to a forward direction in fast flight, either by deflection or other means, thereby tending to increase the forward speed. In a recent project, the tail rotor has been inclined in such a manner as to give lift as well as side thrust. This means that at high forward speed the fuselage will tend to have a more nose-down attitude, consequently an increased amount of forward control is available for attaining even higher speeds.

A neat type of shrouded tail rotor called a *fenestron* is used in the Aérospatiale Gazelle and Dauphin. It reduces the danger of blades striking a person or object on the ground. *Tail rotor* is, perhaps, a misnomer for it has more resemblance to a ducted fan.

At least one six-bladed tail rotor has, in order to minimize the overall diameter for a given length of blade, two parallel planes of rotation. One plane is for three of the blades and the other for the remainder which are spaced equally between the first three blades.

An unusual tail-rotor configuration is used for anti-resonant purposes in the Hughes Advanced Attack Helicopter. The four blades are mounted at 60° and 120° instead of the normal 90°.

The testing and checking of rotor systems and rotor blades has been advanced by the use of rotor spinning towers, the first of which was designed by Hafner in 1945. These enable blade behaviour to be studied or corrected with the most advanced resources available. Towers can be supplemented by tethered ground running of the complete helicopter and, apart from those which can only be used in flight, almost every system can be tested.

Pilots' Controls

In the first few years after the development of the practical helicopter, the cyclic-pitch stick and the collective-pitch lever were directly connected to the pitch-change mechanism of the rotor blades, and it was the pilot's strength alone which altered the blade pitch. The linkage was through systems designed to require the minimum of physical strength and to be partly irreversible. If the cyclic-pitch stick were released it would, depending on aircraft type, describe an orbit or fall to one side. Friction devices could be used to prevent this. Alternatively, trimmers could be used: these started with home-made systems such as bungees fitted directly to the stick and developed to electrically operated mechanisms operating on the control linkage.

The introduction of servo controls to all but the smallest helicopters was a great improvement and the pilot is now required to exert only a minute control force. Since a leverage advantage was no longer necessary, the collective-pitch lever in particular could be made more sensitive and the movement of the control through its full range could be reduced to about one third of the original travel for the same effect on the blades.

An initial disadvantage of powered controls was that in the event of servo failure the strength required to fly the aircraft in manual control was much greater than hitherto, for aids such as screw jacks in the control system had been removed. It was acknowledged that a second independent servo system was required to overcome what could be a hazardous situation. The next logical step was to give spring feel to the cyclic-pitch stick and where this was done the datum could be adjusted by electrically operated trimmers.

For rudder control, powered systems are generally coupled with a damper to prevent sudden large forces being supplied by the tail rotor.

With the introduction of gas-turbine engines, the normal control of the engine by twist-grip throttle was changed to automatic control. The twist-grip was often retained, however, as an r.p.m. select control or as an emergency manual throttle.

For deck landing, some helicopters have been given a special collective-pitch facility to enable the lever to be lowered beyond its normal limits. This is called *superfine* pitch and can be used in conjunction with a harpoon decklock system to attach the aircraft firmly to the deck. In the Lynx helicopter the facility is increased by enabling the blades to enter into the negative pitch range. Another method of deck landing and deck attachment is the Bear Trap: a cable is lowered from the helicopter while it is hovering and a winch pulls the aircraft right down onto the deck. Similar to this is the R.A.S.T. (Recover Assist Secure and Traverse) which additionally involves a sideways movement into the ship's hangar after landing.

Ground simulators for specific helicopter types have been developed and have been used for pilot familiarization and for training and practice in the use of aircraft systems.

Maintenance

Considerable improvements have been made. In general the number of component parts has been reduced. Rotor heads are generally less complex, with flapping and drag hinges superseded in some cases by bending elements which are flexible in the required planes, thus eliminating the need for lubrication. The heavy centrifugal loads which used to be borne by pitch-change bearings may now be carried by torsionally flexible tie bars. In this case, if the pitch-change bearings are retained, they can consist of easily maintained journal bearings.

Main components have been made more easily changeable.

Irksome tasks, such as tracking, have been made simpler and a good track will last longer by virtue of improved rotor blades.

The use of conformal gears has not only cut down the number of stages necessary for speed reduction, but also the number of bearings and components. These gears offer a potential reduction in the weight of the gear boxes. In essence, the gear-tooth form of conformal gearing is based on circular arcs instead of involute curves so that the area in contact between teeth is much greater. This is claimed to improve lubrication and load capacity.

Improvements in test methods and metallurgy have made it possible to predict lives more accurately, thus enabling longer safe lives to be declared.

The necessity for using tools such as the grease gun has been reduced by having bearings which can be lubricated by small oil reservoirs and which have visible oil levels. In some cases, the use of elastomeric bearings has eliminated the need for lubrication altogether.

One of the features most appreciated has been the way in which components have been made more accessible. For example, instead of clumsy interlocking cowlings there are hinged panels and door-type handles.

Vibration

There has been considerable research into the vibration problem. Early helicopters suffered considerably from this trouble and improvements have come with the arrival of rotor blades which do not vary in stiffness, pitching moments, damper settings and balance. Vibration from sources such as engines, drive shafts, gear boxes, etc., has been reduced. The use of gas turbines instead of piston engines has also helped. Unfortunately, the overall improvement has been partially offset by the fact that helicopter speeds have tended to be higher, so new problems have arisen and old ones have tended to become more prominent.

Ways of reducing the effect of rotor vibrations on the fuselage have been sought. Among these, mass absorbers have been adopted and often the aircraft battery has been used as the mass in order to avoid an excessive weight penalty. This method is generally most effective at one rotor speed, however, and it does not benefit the whole airframe. A recent innovation is the adaptation of the bifiler pendulum absorber (Plate IV). As applied to the rotor it consists of a number of arms, corresponding to the number of blades, each of which carries a loosely attached weight. The weights oscillate in response to vibrations in such a way that they tend to oppose the rotor vibration forces and prevent them being transmitted to the airframe. The system is effective at any rotor speed.

Another vibration-reducing system used by Bell is nodal beam (or Noda-matic) suspension. The beam is interposed between the gearbox and the airframe attachment points situated at the node point of the vibrating beam. The vibration from the rotor is absorbed by the beam leaving its mounting relatively motionless.

Automatic Pilots

Instrument flying has developed at a steady pace, British European Airways being pioneers in this field from 1948. The handling of a helicopter under instrument conditions required considerable practice and the arrival of aids to help the pilot was a welcome breakthrough. Automatic stabilization equipment was developed in the 1950s and with this the helicopter could be flown without the pilot touching the controls, but he could use the controls at any time to carry out manoeuvres.

A further advance was a linkage between the autopilot and a Doppler Radar system that enabled the helicopter to carry out completely automatic approaches to the hover; to hold a hover over land or water; and to climb away to a pre-determined height, thus enhancing the role of the helicopter in anti-submarine warfare. Over water the ability to carry out automatic station-keeping over a sonar buoy was a further refinement.

A recent development is an autostabilizer utilizing fluidics. (Fluidics is the science and technology of using a flow of liquid or gas for certain operations instead of a flow of electrons.) Amplifiers using compressed air tapped from the engine(s) replace the conventional electronic amplifier.

Development in automatic approaches and landings by flying down radio beams parallels the progress made with similar systems for fixed-wing aircraft.

Payloads

Early helicopters such as the R.4 could scarcely hover in the ground cushion on a hot, calm day with one passenger aboard. Nowadays, it is accepted as normal that even the smallest helicopter should be able to climb vertically from the ground, have a hovering ceiling of several thousand feet out of ground effect, and carry a useful payload as well. Whereas the payload in the early days might consist of one or two passengers, whose dimensions the pilot might scan anxiously as they embarked, the modern helicopter can cope not only with internal loads, but also external ones, either fixed to the fuselage or slung. The increase in load-carrying ability is a good indication of the way in which the helicopter has progressed from an early experimental machine to a vehicle of vast potential. From a payload of 100 kg or so in the 1930s and early 1940s the record load has risen from 20,117 kg in 1959 to 40,204 kg in 1969.

Performance

An indication of the improvement can be seen by the following:

World speed records have increased from 122.5 km/h in 1937, to 200 km/h in 1948 and 356 km/h in 1970.

The world height record has increased from 5,842 metres in 1937, to 6,468 metres in 1949 and 12,440 metres in 1972.

Minimizing Battle Damage

In recent years, attention has been directed towards minimizing the effect of battle damage on military helicopters so that even if the aircraft is hit by gunfire it still has a good chance of returning to friendly territory.

Blades have been built to withstand the effect of hits by small-calibre shells. More recently, blades have been of multi-spar construction so that damage to one spar will not result in catastrophic failure. Large tail surfaces ensure that forward-powered flight is still possible with the tail rotor unserviceable. Armour, either metal or plastic, has been used not only to protect the crew but vulnerable parts of the helicopter as well. In twin-engined types, the positioning of the engines athwart the fuselage affords a certain amount of protection for one engine in the event of a side attack. Wide spacing of the engines also reduces the chance of a single hit damaging both engines. Bearings in oil-filled gear boxes have been mounted in plastic so as to delay failure if the gear box is holed; better still is the development of gear boxes which use grease instead of oil. Twin- and multi-engined helicopters are more reliable than single-engined ones. The development of fly-by-wire systems of control, in which control commands are transmitted to the actuator position by cables following many different routes, means that damage to a few cables does not cause loss of control. (There is also a weight saving, especially in large helicopters.)

For minimizing the possibility of hits by enemy fire, some attention has been paid to the use of low radar profiles. To lessen the possibility of strikes by infra-red and heat-seeking missiles, shielding has been used round exhaust pipes, and exhaust gases are cooled by mixing with ambient air before discharge.

Economics

Helicopters have suffered, and are still suffering, from the fact that the initial capital cost is high. This is due to the expense of development, which manufacturers attempt to recover from the aircraft that they sell; and the fact that the helicopter has many moving parts, all of which must have the utmost integrity.

If the capital cost of the machine is written off after only a few years, then depreciation is shown in the profit-and-loss account as a substantial item and the operating costs per hour can appear unduly large. Man hours spent on maintenance have shown a marked reduction, but there remains the fact that in many helicopters expensive "lifted" items, such as rotor blades, have to be replaced and this again has an effect on the operating costs. Recent improvements in rotor-head and rotor-blade design, however, should have an increasingly beneficial effect especially on small and medium-sized helicopters. Certain flying tasks call for an increase in the insurance premium and can also inflate costs.

The price of the basic aircraft may tend to improve owing to the reduction in the number of parts, brought about by improved technology. Operating costs should be helped by further improvements, bringing about a reduction in the man-hours necessary for maintenance. Where, however, sophisticated equipment is purchased with the aircraft the necessary capital outlay is considerably increased.

It makes sense to use a helicopter only where no other vehicle can compete in the time available. Helicopters are, therefore, found doing tasks in places inaccessible to other vehicles and/or where time is valuable. On the other hand, very small helicopters and gyroplanes can often be operated at a comparatively reasonable rate for pleasure or for tasks requiring only small payloads; the convenience of being able to land almost anywhere gives them an advantage over small fixed-wing aircraft.

QUESTIONNAIRE

1. What is meant by: (*a*) an articulated rotor (*b*) a semi-rigid rotor (*c*) a rigid rotor?
2. Describe six helicopter configurations.
3. Name the pilot's controls.
4. Give four possible positions for engine locations in a helicopter.
5. What types of undercarriage can be used?
6. How is the overall thrust of a rotor normally varied by the pilot?
7. In a hovering helicopter what is the relationship between lift and weight?
8. How can rotor blades be constructed in order to give an approximately constant inflow of air along the span?
9. What is the purpose of the throttle cam?
10. What do you understand by static droop?
11. What do you understand by transient droop?
12. How does a helicopter move forward from the hover?
13. Describe the tachometer as fitted in helicopters.
14. What has happened to the clutch when the tachometer needles become superimposed?
15. What is meant by "splitting the needles"?
16. What is meant by the rotor disc?
17. What is meant by rotor disc attitude?
18. What is the difference between cyclic pitch and collective pitch?
19. What is the difference in the fuselage attitude when hovering and when in cruising flight?
20. What is meant by the advancing blade?
21. What does movement of the stick do to the rotor blades when the rotor is stopped?
22. What is meant by flapping?
23. What is meant by the phase lag, and what is the approximate phase lag angle in an articulated rotor system?
24. What is meant by off-setting the flapping hinges?
25. How does off-setting the flapping hinges affect the phase lag?
26. Describe the function of the swash plate.

27. Describe in detail how the rotor disc is tilted forward for forward flight.
28. Why is lift lost when the stick is eased forward in the hover?
29. How does a tandem rotor helicopter move forward?
30. What two main factors affect the top speed of helicopters?
31. Why does the fitting of fixed wings to a helicopter permit greater speeds?
32. What does torque reaction tend to do to the fuselage of a helicopter in which the rotor is shaft-driven?
33. How can the torque reaction be balanced in single-rotor helicopters?
34. How can torque reaction be balanced in multi-rotor helicopters?
35. In which direction does the aircraft turn when left rudder is applied in the hover?
36. Why is a considerable amount of rudder necessary to hold a straight autorotational glide?
37. Assuming right rudder is being held in a straight auto-rotational glide, what happens to the pitch of the tail rotor when full right rudder is applied?
38. If left rudder is being held to keep straight in hovering flight, what happens to the r.p.m. if more left rudder is applied?
39. The rail rotor tends to move the helicopter sideways in hovering flight. How is this drift prevented?
40. Why does a helicopter often hover with a lateral tilt?
41. What force acting on rotor blades tends to make them cone upwards in flight?
42. What limits the degree of coning in flight?
43. What is meant by the coning angle?
44. How does the coning angle of a helicopter rotor hovering at 1,000 ft in calm air compare with that of a similar helicopter hovering at 10,000 ft in calm air, assuming the same rotor r.p.m. and all-up weight are used?
45. What is meant by over-pitching?
46. In what conditions of aircraft all-up weight and air density is a pilot more likely to over-pitch?
47. How should a pilot correct the over-pitched condition?
48. What is meant by translational lift?
49. Is it possible to experience translational lift when hovering?

50. What is meant by the ground effect?
51. When is the ground cushion of particular value?
52. What effect do up-gusts tend to have on the rotor in flight?
53. What do you understand by: (a) Disc loading. (b) Blade loading. (c) Solidity. (d) Power loading?
54. What is meant by "a one per rev." vibration?
55. What is a vibrograph used for?
56. What methods can be used to determine which rotor blades are out of track?
57. What are the differences between a helicopter and a gyroplane in: (a) appearance (b) construction (c) performance?
58. What causes dissymmetry of lift?
59. Owing to dissymmetry of lift the rotor disc tends to tilt back when there is an increase of airspeed. How is this tendency corrected?
60. Define autorotation.
61. Are the rotor blades in high pitch or low pitch in autorotative flight?
62. Why is the engine not turned by the rotor in autorotative flight?
63. What effect does high altitude have on the rotor r.p.m. in autorotative flight?
64. What is meant by dragging?
65. Why do rotor blades tend to move about their drag hinges?
66. What are drag dampers for?
67. What would a pilot experience during ground resonance?
68. How should a pilot correct ground resonance?
69. What aircraft faults and piloting errors tend to induce ground resonance?
70. Why do helicopters tend to be unstable?
71. Assuming constant r.p.m. are maintained, which of the pilot's controls will vary the boost?
72. In hovering manoeuvres which of the pilot's controls is used to control the height?
73. In hovering manoeuvres how is the heading maintained or altered?
74. Unless absolutely necessary, what are the approximate heights above ground between which single-engined helicopters should not be hovered or flown slowly?

75. Describe the respective functions of the pilot's controls when flying sideways.
76. Describe the effect of a wind on the helicopter during a turn on the spot.
77. What flight conditions and manoeuvres tend to induce blade stall?
78. What does a pilot experience during blade stall?
79. What methods can be used to recover from blade stall?
80. What are the two main problems associated with steep approaches to small sites?
81. What are the conditions necessary to induce the vortex ring condition?
82. What will the pilot experience during flight in the vortex ring condition?
83. How can a pilot recover from the vortex ring condition?
84. What should the pilot's immediate action be in the event of an engine failure in cruising flight?
85. What control has the pilot over the helicopter in auto-rotative flight?
86. How does a pilot prevent an unwanted rise in rotor r.p.m. during autorotative flight?
87. How can the airspeed be used to control the glide path during an autorotative descent?
88. How do the rotor r.p.m. affect the glide path during an autorotative descent?
89. What two methods can be used to stop the downward motion when in autorotation?
90. What effect does a flare have on the rotor r.p.m.?
91. Describe an engine-off landing in which both methods of stopping the downward motion are used.
92. What method can be used to become airborne when the helicopter has insufficient power to take off vertically?
93. When flying at maximum available power above the full throttle height how are the r.p.m. controlled?
94. How does the minimum airspeed to maintain height at maximum power vary with altitude?
95. Why does the maximum airspeed decrease with increased altitude?
96. What effect does altitude have on the sensitivity of the controls?
97. Will the rotor r.p.m. in autorotation tend to be higher or lower at high altitudes compared with lower levels?

98. Describe how the pilot would maintain the correct rotor r.p.m. during a descent from high altitude in autorotation.
99. Under what conditions can a helicopter fly level for several seconds in autorotation?
100. What change, if any, should take place in the altitude during a quick stop?

EXTENDED CAPTIONS TO THE PHOTOGRAPHS

Plate I. Juan de la Cierva, 1895–1936. (*Royal Aeronautical Society*)

Plate II. Igor Sikorsky, 1889–1972. (*Flight International*)

Plate III. The rotor head of a large helicopter, the Westland Sea King. The mechanism is more complex than in most helicopters owing to the powered blade-folding system which is incorporated. (*Westland Aircraft*)

Plate IV. One of the bifilar pendulum absorber arms mounted experimentally on the rotor head of a Lynx helicopter (*Westland Aircraft*)

Plate V. The Sikorsky R.4 (185 h.p. Warner-Scarab engine) was the first helicopter in the world to be produced in any number. The first of the few dozen to be used by British forces arrived in Britain in 1944. Called the "Gadfly" by the Royal Navy and the "Hoverfly I" by the R.A.F., it is remembered with affection by the author, although by today's standards its characteristics would be considered crude. The top of the cyclic-pitch stick tended to describe an orbit during flight. The vibration level was generally high. The power was such that on a hot, calm day the aircraft could only just hover in the ground cushion at maximum all-up weight; so dexterity was needed to move forward to gain translational lift. Early models had separate tachometers for rotor and engine r.p.m. instead of superimposed needles in one instrument. Flight in heavy rain was not advised, as the tips of the fabric-covered rotor blades could be damaged. Despite its shortcomings, the R.4 did some useful work and demonstrated the potential of the helicopter. (*Flight*)

Plate VI. The S.51 (500 h.p. Alvis Leonides engine) was built by Westland Aircraft Ltd. under licence from Sikorsky Aircraft. Known as the Dragonfly, it was the first helicopter to be used in any number by the Royal Navy and R.A.F. It carried a pilot and three passengers and provision could be made for external loads on winch or sling. On the civil side the S.51 was used for crop spraying, passenger carrying, film work and pilot training. Several were used by the whaling industry and operated from factory ships to spot whales. B.E.A. used the American-built Sikorsky S.51 for a variety of experimental work such as mail carrying, scheduled services with passengers, instrument flying and pilot training. (*Westland Aircraft*)

Plate VII. The Westland Widgeon (500 h.p. Alvis Leonides engine) was a development of the Dragonfly. The centre section and tail of the Dragonfly were retained, but the rotor head was of the type used in the Whirlwind. The cockpit and cabin were redesigned enabling a pilot and four passengers to be carried. Dual controls with side-by-side seating for instructor and pupil were available for pilot training. The aircraft was used primarily as a training aircraft or as a passenger transport but some were exported to foreign air forces. (*Westland Aircraft*)

Plate VIII. There were several versions of the Westland Whirlwind. The latest, shown here, is the gas-turbine-powered model. The Gnome engine is controlled by an electronic computer so that in powered flight the rotor r.p.m. are automatically controlled. Flight with a manually operated twist-grip throttle is also possible. Civil Whirlwinds have been widely used for passenger-carrying and charter work and in particular for transporting men and materials to oil rigs. Perhaps the best-known use to which military Whirlwinds have been put is rescue work. Earlier Whirlwinds were fitted with Pratt and Whitney Wasp, Wright Cyclone, or Leonides Major engines. (*Westland Aircraft*)

Plate IX. The Westland Wessex has been produced in several versions. This one, operating in the jungles of Borneo, is the Mark V and has two Gnome gas-turbine engines. In powered flight the rotor r.p.m. are automatically controlled by electronic computers, no manual throttle control being available. Sixteen fully-armed troops or alternative loads can be carried.

The civil version of twin-Gnome Wessex, the Wessex 60, is operated by Bristow Helicopters Ltd. to drilling rigs in the North Sea. (*Westland Aircraft*)

Plate X.   This Westland-built Augusta-Bell 47G–3B–1 (270 b.p.h. Lycoming engine) is called the "Sioux" by the army and is one of a long and successful series of Bell helicopters. An unusual feature of this model is the supercharger which is driven by exhaust gases, enabling performance to be maintained to comparatively high altitudes. A safety feature is the high inertia rotor which makes engine-off landings easier. This particular model is a military one, but it is helicopters of this size that have been widely used for crop dusting and crop spraying and for executive and personal transport. (*Westland Aircraft*)

Plate XI.   The Westland Belvedere is shown landing at the Battersea Heliport, London. Two Gazelle gas-turbine engines power the tandem rotors and flight could be maintained on one engine if necessary. Nineteen fully-equipped troops, or alternative loads such as twelve stretcher cases, could be carried. (*Westland Aircraft*)

Plate XII.   This Sikorsky S61N is one of the helicopters being operated by British Airways on scheduled services between Penzance and the Scilly Isles. Twenty-eight passengers can be carried at a cruising speed of 120 knots. The two General Electric T58 gas-turbine engines can be seen mounted above the fuselage. The flying-boat hull is a safety factor in the event of a forced landing in the sea. (*Westland Aircraft*)

Plate XIII.   The Westland-built Sea King is powered by two Gnome G.1400 free-turbine engines and has been ordered not only by the Royal Navy and the R.A.F. but also by the forces of Australia, Belgium, Germany, India, Pakistan, Norway and the Middle East. Its wide range of roles include anti-submarine duties, and search and rescue. It can lift 24 passengers or up to an 8,000 lb payload. The main rotor blades can be folded or spread by the pilot without assistance from the ground crew. The troop-carrying version of this aircraft is the Commando which can carry 34 fully-equipped troops. (*Westland Aircraft*)

Plate XIV.   Westland Helicopters and Aérospatiale of France collaborated in the building of the Lynx, with Westland as the design leader. The aircraft is used by British and French forces for training, anti-submarine work and general purpose and utility. It is powered by two Rolls Royce RS 360 free-turbine engines. This aircraft holds the world speed record for its class of 321.74 km/h over a straight course. (*Westland Aircraft*)

Plate XV. The Puma, or S.A.330, is another example of British-French collaboration. Designed in France, the aircraft is built in both countries and is used by the R.A.F. for tactical transport. Sixteen men and their equipment can be carried. It is powered by two Turbomeca Turmo IV free-turbine engines. (*Westland Aircraft*)

Plate XVI. The Gazelle, or S.A.341, is also a product of British-French collaboration. The engine is an Astazou III, which is a fixed-shaft turbine. The most noticeable feature is the shrouded tail rotor or fenestron which reduces the danger to people on the ground and lessens the possiblity of damage by trees or shrubs. An infinite life is claimed for the rotor blades. The Gazelle has gained three international speed records for its class. (*Westland Aircraft*)

GLOSSARY

The following terms are not specifically defined in the text and the definitions may be of value to readers.

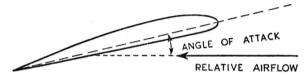

FIG. 106. ANGLE OF ATTACK

ANGLE OF ATTACK. The acute angle between the chord line of a rotor blade and the relative airflow (Fig. 106).

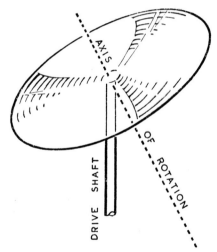

FIG. 107. AXIS OF ROTATION

ANGLE OF INCIDENCE. A term not used in this book as people sometimes use it in the sense of *angle of attack* and sometimes in the sense of *pitch angle*.

AXIAL FLOW. That component flow of air through a rotor which is normal to the tip-path plane.

AXIS OF ROTATION. An imaginary line which passes through

a point about which a body rotates and which is normal
to the plane of rotation (Fig. 107).

CENTRE OF GRAVITY. The point in a body through which
the resultant of the weights of its parts passes, whatever
position it may assume.

CENTRE OF PRESSURE. That point on an aerofoil where the
resultant of all aerodynamic forces may be assumed to act.

COMPONENT. See *Resultant and Component.*

CONTROL ADVANCE ANGLE. The horizontal angle measured at
the rotor centre between the spanwise axis of a blade and the
point of attachment of its push-pull rods (control horns,
control arms, etc.) to the swash plate (spider, etc.).

DRAG. That component of the resultant of the aerodynamic

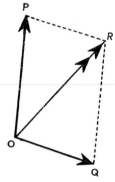

FIG. 108. PARALLELOGRAM OF FORCES

forces acting on a body which acts parallel to the relative
airflow.

FORCE. A force is any influence which changes or tends to
change the state of rest or uniform motion of a body.

LIFT. That component of the resultant of the aerodynamic
forces acting on a body which acts at right angles to the
relative airflow.

PARALLELOGRAM OF FORCES. If two forces acting from a point
be represented in magnitude, direction and sense by two
sides of a parallelogram drawn from one of its angular
points, their resultant is represented in magnitude, direction
and sense by the diagonal of the parallelogram passing
through that angular point (Fig. 108).

In the figure, *OP* and *OQ* are vectors representing forces acting from position *O*. By making *OP* and *OQ* two sides of a parallelogram, and by drawing in parallel lines (dotted), we can find the resultant of *OP* and *OQ*.

PITCH ANGLE or PITCH. The acute angle between the chord of a rotor blade and a reference surface on the rotor hub (Fig. 109). This reference surface is usually normal to the drive shaft.

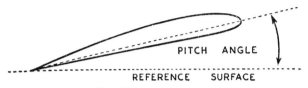

FIG. 109. PITCH ANGLE

PLANE OF ROTATION or TIP-PATH PLANE. A plane formed by the average tip-path of the rotor blades and which is normal to the axis of rotation (Fig. 110).

RELATIVE AIRFLOW. The velocity of the air with reference to a body in it.

Relative AIRFLOW is opposite in sense to that of the flight path of the body being referred to.

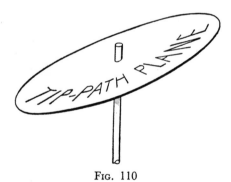

FIG. 110

RESULTANT and COMPONENT. If two or more forces act on a rigid body, and if a single force can be found whose effect upon the body is the same as that of these forces, then the single force is called the *resultant* and the original forces are called the *components* of that force.

In Fig. 108 *P* and *Q* are two forces acting about a point *O*. *OR* is the resultant of the two forces (resultants are usually marked with a double-headed arrow) and *OP* and *OQ* are the components.

TIP-SPEED RATIO. The ratio between the forward speed of the aircraft and the rotational speed of the rotor-blade tip.

TRANSLATIONAL FLIGHT. A horizontal motion of an aircraft through the air irrespective of the heading of the aircraft.

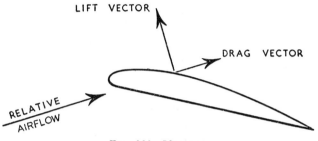

FIG. 111. VECTORS

VECTOR. A straight line drawn to represent the magnitude, direction and sense of a quantity such as a force or velocity.

Magnitude is represented by the length of the line, i.e. if the magnitude of a force is five pounds, the line is drawn five units (inches, feet, centimetres, etc.) long. Direction is represented by the angle the line makes to some axis, and by marking the line with an arrow the sense of a force can be represented.

Well-known examples of a vector are lift and drag vectors (Fig. 111).

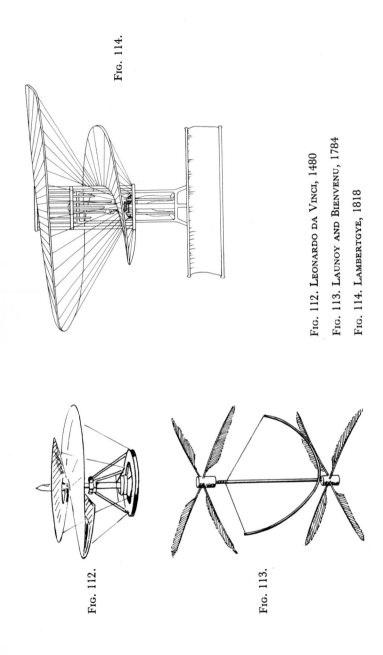

FIG. 114.

FIG. 112. LEONARDO DA VINCI, 1480

FIG. 113. LAUNOY AND BIENVENU, 1784

FIG. 114. LAMBERTGYE, 1818

FIG. 112.

FIG. 113.

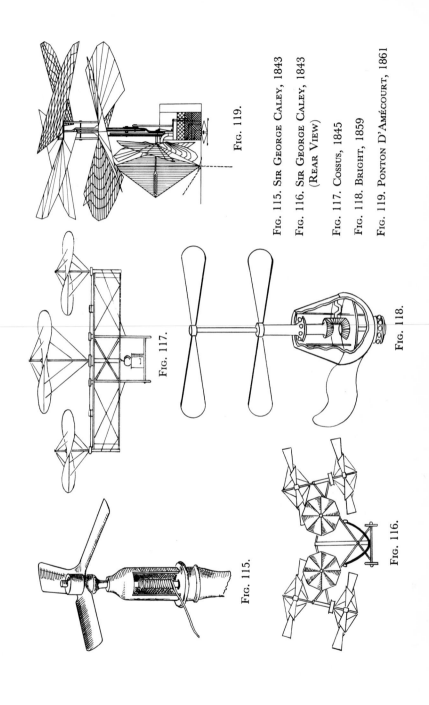

FIG. 119.

FIG. 115. SIR GEORGE CALEY, 1843

FIG. 116. SIR GEORGE CALEY, 1843
(REAR VIEW)

FIG. 117. COSSUS, 1845

FIG. 118. BRIGHT, 1859

FIG. 119. PONTON D'AMÉCOURT, 1861

FIG. 117.

FIG. 118.

FIG. 115.

FIG. 116.

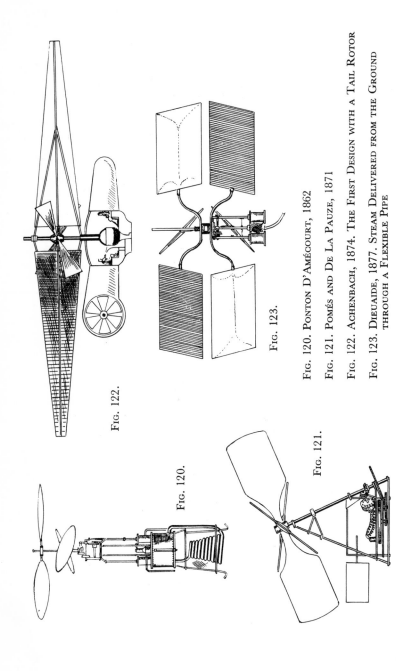

Fig. 120. Ponton D'Amécourt, 1862

Fig. 121. Pomés and De La Pauze, 1871

Fig. 122. Achenbach, 1874. The First Design with a Tail Rotor

Fig. 123. Dieuaide, 1877. Steam Delivered from the Ground through a Flexible Pipe

Fig. 120.

Fig. 121.

Fig. 122.

Fig. 123.

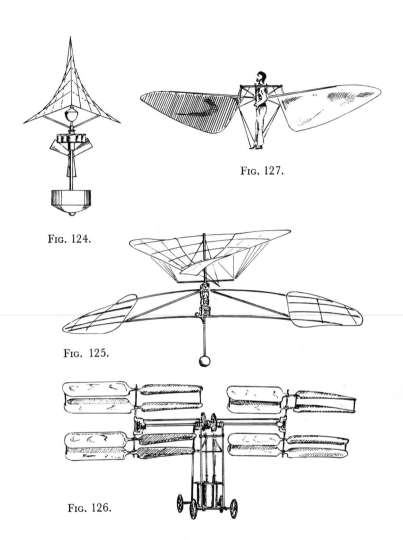

FIG. 124.

FIG. 127.

FIG. 125.

FIG. 126.

FIG. 124. MELIKOFF, 1877

FIG. 125. FORLANINI, 1877. FIRST SHAFT-DRIVEN, STEAM-POWERED MODEL
HELICOPTER TO LEAVE THE GROUND.

FIG. 126. CASTEL, 1877

FIG. 127. DANDRIEUX, 1879

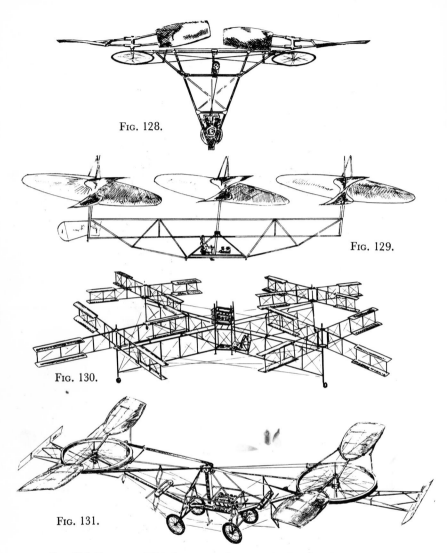

Fig. 128.

Fig. 129.

Fig. 130.

Fig. 131.

FIG. 128. RENARD, 1904. INTERNAL COMBUSTION ENGINE. FLAPPING
     HINGES

FIG. 129. DENNY, 1906–14

FIG. 130. BREGUET-RICHET No. 1, 1907

FIG. 131. CORNU, 1907

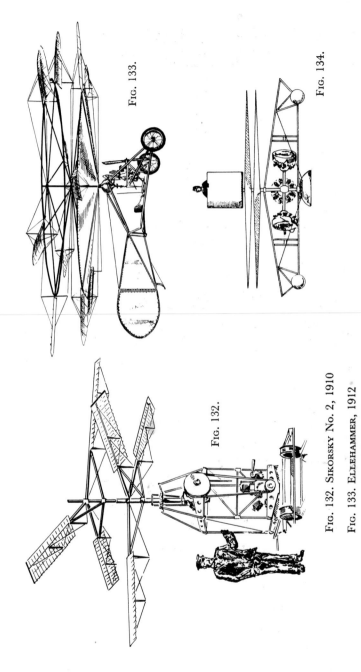

Fig. 133.

Fig. 134.

Fig. 132.

Fig. 132. Sikorsky No. 2, 1910

Fig. 133. Ellehammer, 1912

Fig. 134. Karman-Petrosczy, 1916. Observation Machine. Tethered Flight Only.

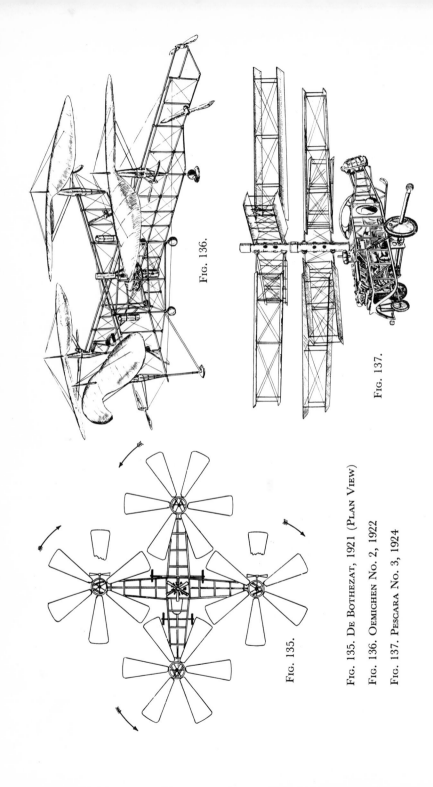

FIG. 136.

FIG. 137.

FIG. 135.

FIG. 135. DE BOTHEZAT, 1921 (PLAN VIEW)

FIG. 136. OEMICHEN NO. 2, 1922

FIG. 137. PESCARA NO. 3, 1924

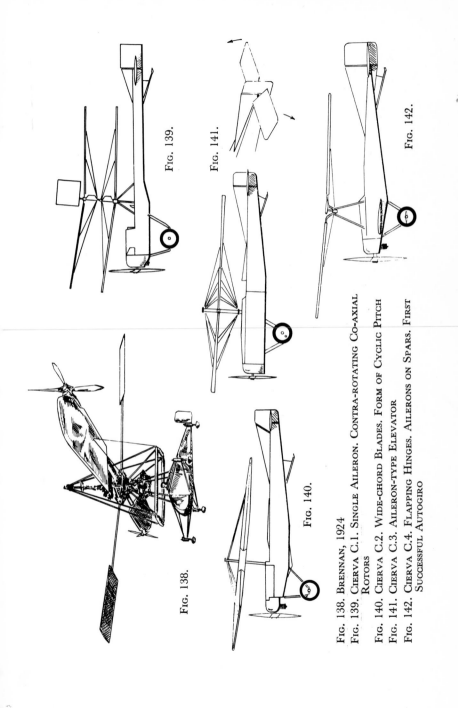

FIG. 139.

FIG. 141.

FIG. 142.

FIG. 140.

FIG. 138.

Fig. 138. Brennan, 1924

Fig. 139. Cierva C.1. Single Aileron. Contra-rotating Co-axial
Rotors

Fig. 140. Cierva C.2. Wide-chord Blades. Form of Cyclic Pitch

Fig. 141. Cierva C.3. Aileron-type Elevator

Fig. 142. Cierva C.4. Flapping Hinges. Ailerons on Spars. First
Successful Autogiro

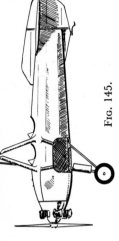

Fig. 143.

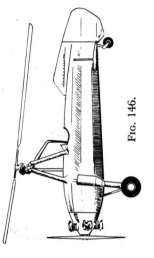

Fig. 144.

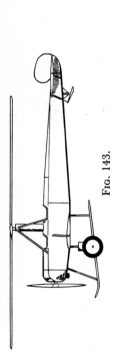

Fig. 145.

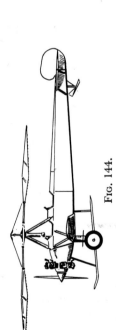

Fig. 146.

Note: There were several variants of each Cierva aircraft.

Fig. 143. Cierva C.6. Demonstrated in Britain

Fig. 144. Cierva C.8. Built in Britain

Fig. 145. Cierva C.19 Mark IV. Rotor Starting by Engine Drive through a Clutch

Fig. 146. Cierva C.19 Mark V. No Wings. Experimental Direct Control

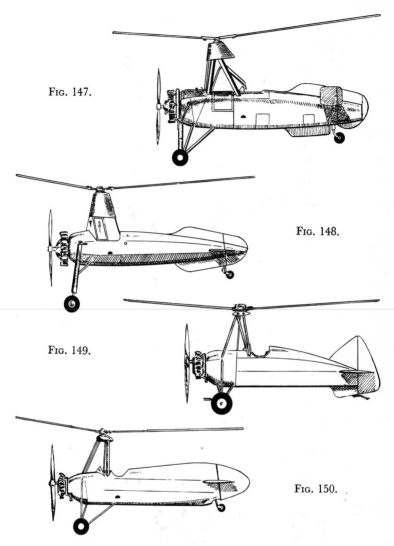

FIG. 147.

FIG. 148.

FIG. 149.

FIG. 150.

FIG. 147. CIERVA C.30 OR ROTA I. FIRST PRODUCTION MODEL WITH
DIRECT CONTROL
FIG. 148. CIERVA C.40 OR ROTA II. JUMP TAKE-OFF AUTOGIRO
FIG. 149. KAY GYROPLANE, 1932
FIG. 150. HAFNER GYROPLANE A.R.III, 1935. JUMP TAKE-OFF
CAPABILITY WITH PILOT-CONTROLLED COLLECTIVE PITCH

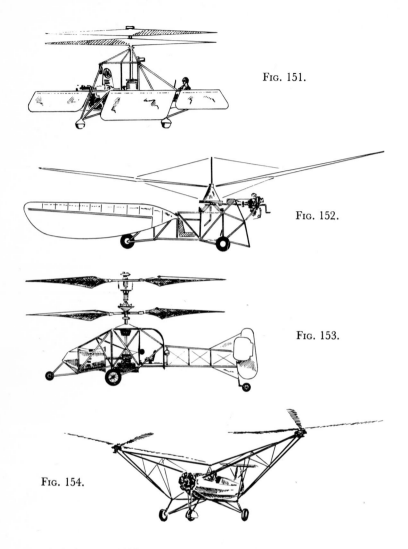

Fig. 151.

Fig. 152.

Fig. 153.

Fig. 154.

Fig. 151. Asboth, 1928

Fig. 152. Hafner R.II, 1932

Fig. 153. Breguet-Dorand, 1933

Fig. 154. Fw 61, 1936. World's First Practical Helicopter

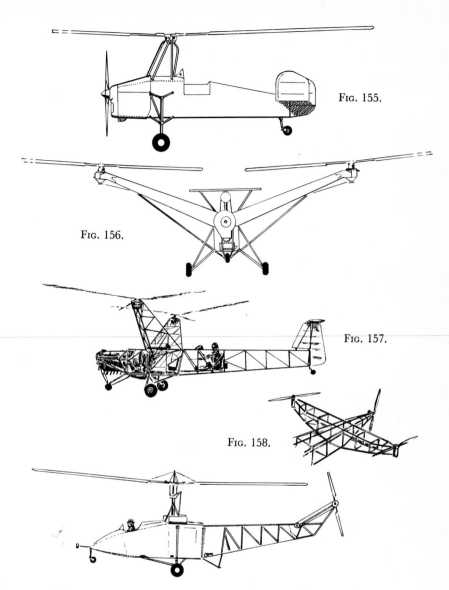

FIG. 155. WEIR W.3, 1936. TWO-BLADED JUMP TAKE-OFF GYROPLANE
FIG. 156. WEIR W.5, 1938. FIRST SUCCESSFUL BRITISH HELICOPTER
FIG. 157. WEIR W.6, 1939. WORLD'S FIRST TWO-SEAT HELICOPTER
FIG. 158. SIKORSKY VS 300, 1939. THE SMALLER FIGURE SHOWS ONE OF
    THE TAIL CONFIGURATIONS USED EXPERIMENTALLY

FIG. 159.

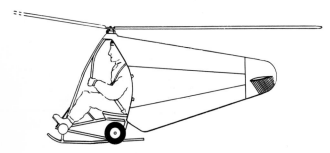

FIG. 160.

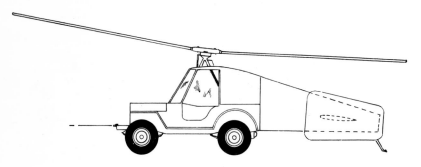

FIG. 161.

FIG. 159. FLETTNER FL.282 (KOLIBRI), 1941

FIG. 160. ROTACHUTE MK. 3, 1942. AN AUTOGYRO GLIDER

FIG. 161. ROTABUGGY, 1943. AN AUTOGYRO GLIDER

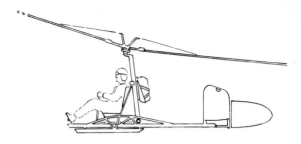

Fig. 162.

Fig. 163.

Fig. 164.

Fig. 162. Fa 330, 1942. German Autogyro Kite which was Towed by a Submarine

Fig. 163. Doblhoff WNF 342 V2, 1943. First Helicopter to use Tip-jet Drive successfully

Fig. 164. Doblhoff WNF 343 V4, 1945. Tip-jet Drive for Helicopter Flight. Converted to Autogyro for Forward Flight

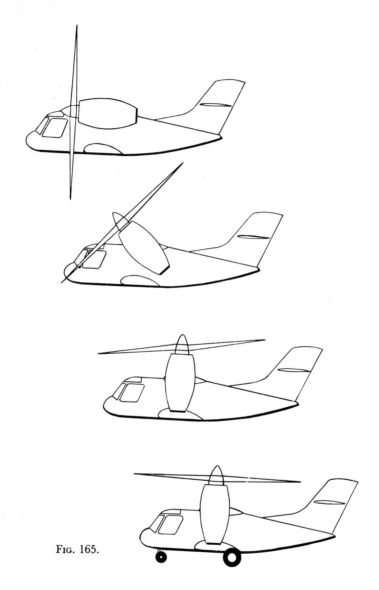

Fig. 165.

Fig. 165. A Tilt-rotor Aircraft. From Bottom to Top: Take-off.
Helicopter Flight. Transition to Cruising Flight. Flight
as a Fixed-wing Aircraft

BIBLIOGRAPHY

[1]. *Science and Civilisation in China*, by Joseph Needham (Cambridge University Press 1965)
[2]. *Aviation*, by Charles H. Gibbs-Smith (Her Majesty's Stationery Office 1970)
[3]. *Helicopters and other Rotorcraft since 1907*, by Kenneth Munson (Blandford Press 1973)
[4]. *A Historical Review of Helicopter Development*, by R. N. Liptrot (Bulletin of H.A.G.B. 1947)
[5]. *Helicopter Research and Development*, by C. G. Pullin (Bulletin of H.A.G.B. 1947)

From *The Journal of The Helicopter Association of Great Britain:*
[6]. "Some Problems of Helicopter Operation and Their Influence on Design", by R. A. C. Brie (1947)
[7]. "Limitations of Helicopter Design", by J. A. J. Bennett (1947)
[8]. "Sikorsky Helicopter Developments", by Igor Sikorsky (1947)
[9]. "Some Work with Rotary Wing Aircraft", by O. L. L. Fitzwilliams (1947)
[10]. "Jet Propulsion of Rotor Blades", by A. Stepan (1949)
[11]. "Some Economics of the Helicopter, Present and Future", by L. S. Wigdortchik (1949)
[12]. "A Bibliography of Rotary Wing Aircraft", by Bennett and Liptrot (1950)
[13]. "Convertible Aircraft", by R. N. Liptrot (1951)
[14]. "The Giant Helicopter", by O. L. L. Fitzwilliams (1952)
[15]. "A Review of Helicopter Patents", by L. H. Hayward (1952)
[16]. "Canadian Research in the Field of Helicopter Icing", by J. R. Stallibrass (1958)

From *The Royal Aeronautical Society Journal:*
[17]. "The Development of the Autogiro", by Cierva (1926)
[18]. "The Helicopter Rotor", by J. P. Jones (1970)
[19]. "Contributions of the Bell Helicopter Co. to Helicopter Development", by Bartram Kelly (1972)

[20].   *Avro Aircraft since 1908*, by A. J. Jackson (Putnam 1968)
[21].   *Encyclopaedia of Aviation*, by C. G. Burge (Pitman, 1935)
[22].   *Helicopters and Autogyros of the World*, by Lambermont & Pirie (Cassell 1970)
[23].   *Rotorcraft*, by Liptrot and Woods (Butterworths Scientific Publications 1969)
[24].   *Jane's All the World's Aircraft* (Sampson Low, Marston and Co. Ltd Periodic)
[25].   *Flight* and *Flight International*

KEY TO ABBREVIATIONS

The following abbreviations do not necessarily pertain to the subject matter discussed in the book, but may prove useful to readers.

AAH   Advanced Attack Helicopter
ABC   Advancing Blade Concept
AFCS   Automatic Flight Control System
AHS   American Helicopter Society
ARCADS A Lightweight Armament Control and Delivery System
ASH   Advanced Scout Helicopter
ASI   Airspeed Indicator
ASW   Anti-submarine Warfare
ATAFCS Airborne Target Acquisition Fire Control System
ATW   Anti-tank Warfare
BERP   British Experimental Rotor Programme
BHAB   British Helicopter Advisory Board
BIM   Blade Inspection
CAA   Civil Aviation Authority
CAC   Collective Acceleration Control
CCR   Circulation Control Rotor
CF   Centrifugal Force
CG   Centre of Gravity
FAA   Fleet Air Arm. Federal Aviation Administration
FAS   Force Adjustment System

g In aviation, generally refers to the force, caused by inertia, that acts on an aircraft during manoeuvres and disturbances (1g = the force of gravity, 2g = double the force of gravity). Its action is parallel to the normal axis of the aircraft. Positive g is experienced in pull-ups, steep turns and up-gusts, negative g in push-overs and down-gusts.

HEI   Heli-Europe Industries

HELCIS Helicopter Command Instrument System

HLH   Heavy Lift Helicopter

IAS   Indicated Airspeed

IFR   Instrument Flight Rules

ISIS   Integrated Spar Inspection System

LAMPS   Light Airborne Multi-purpose System

LASSIE   Low Airspeed Sensing and Indicating Equipment

LOH   Light Observation Helicopter

MARS   Mid-air Recovery System

MASH   Manned Anti-submarine Helicopter

MATCH   Manned Anti-submarine Torpedo-carrying Aircraft

MMB   Messerschmitt-Bölkhow-Blohm

NOE   Nap of the Earth

PADS   Position and Azimuth Determining System

RAST   Recovery Assist Secure and Traverse

RPH   Remotely Piloted Helicopter

RPM   Revolutions Per Minute

RPV   Remotely Piloted Vehicle

RSRA   Rotor Systems Research Aircraft

RVR   Reversing Velocity Rotor

SAR   Search and Rescue

STALP   Ship Tethered Aerial Lifting Programme

TTLI   Torque-meter Thermal Load Indicator

UTTAS   Utility Tactical Transport Aircraft System

vertRep   Vertical Replenishment

VDR   Variable Diameter Rotor

VFR   Visual Flight Rules

WAL   Westland Aircraft Ltd.

WHL   Westland Helicopters Ltd.

INDEX